Aftermath

PETER MIDDLETON was born in 1950 and grew up in both England and the United States. After a first degree at Oxford University, he took a PhD at Sheffield University, and studied for a year at SUNY Buffalo. He is the author of a book on masculinity, *The Inward Gaze* (1992) and (with Tim Woods) *Literatures of Memory: History, Time and Space in Postwar Writing* (2000). A book of essays on performance, readership, and consumption in contemporary poetry is forthcoming. His poetry and essays have appeared in magazines in the UK and US, and he is an editor of Torque Press. After lecturing at several universities and polytechnics, he is now a Reader in English at the university in Southampton, England, where he lives with his partner Kate, and children George and Harriet.

Aftermath

PETER MIDDLETON

SALT

PUBLISHED BY SALT PUBLISHING
PO Box 937, Great Wilbraham, Cambridge PDO CB1 5JX United Kingdom
PO Box 202, Applecross, Western Australia 6153

© Peter Middleton, 2003

First published 2003

Printed and bound in the United Kingdom by Lightning Source

Typeset in Swift 9.5 / 13

ISBN 1 876857 63 3 paperback

SP

1 3 5 7 9 8 6 4 2

This book is dedicated to Kate, George, and Harriet.

Contents

Paternalisms

Next Gen

Expressions

Topologies

Acknowledgments

I would like to thank the editors of the magazines and presses where many of these poems appeared, sometimes in earlier versions: *A Purge of Dissidence, Aerial, Avec, Constant Red/ Mingled Damask, Figs, fragmente, North Dakota Quarterly, Object Permanence, Pages, Purge, Temblor, The Many Review, The Paper, West Coast Line.*

Equations

First Thought

The forest wakes me it is an im
age of all tree
above aside and catching my walk
but then a wide grass track
is how to wake
waiting
hoper
owning up to no unthought
image engine
a forest without wakers
sentenceless
riser
the pointing word needs over there's branching
arbitrary tree
morning orders us to
cut
and will they take the middle way
the forest wonders
manning
am
soil water and leaflight green
and then not green
greying to rough
elevated
mage
no elevated is not the word
elevation insists the wood
climb or be blind say the birds of the image
to the wakers the woken the wakeman the

Here Is A Clue

Engined metaphysics blow the other
away, as in beyond the outskirts
of London, even beyond the tube.

I am not only the need of the other
but off-world and dangerously
unsyntaxed before planetfall,

and time over distance is domination
in any machine-made article of
faith, the star-traveller's hull

a way of being in and different
from space, the outward sign
of thought's absence from the shelves

in the hypermarket. A lifetimed
journey to the core of the text's
radioactive hypothesis: the universe

is made of words and those limited
elements are fixed until they shoot
particles, decay, and can be measured

not yonder, but on the prior out
esculent in roots but eschatological
at night, the sphere the author of genesis

wrote in to the usual sacred papers
an unrecognisable language. The feeling
is simple but semantic delay inevitable.

Spare Explanations

1.

Seeing as how the extramental
crumples into those flying buttresses
with a dioptric fuss, any reason
had better be good, if meant.

The spice is smoothing its sides
out of ogive against infra-red
warning instructions to channel flick
approaches to the highest.

Maybe, just maybe, is the defense
negotiator, light enough to soar
past the vector loaded supports bill
up and spectacular. This is society.

2.

This likening of evolutionary algorithms
to a chance at government, Kebles
any retrospective purse. You are my other
and could hit any of those words true.

Isn't is not a word in my vocabulary.
Once stated twice here, where here
might be anywhere, but always folds
the note. Creep. Solitude is rile.

The mind, an event, as if these two
possibilities were married but not to each
other's sex. Work that one out.
Real time reproduces well, false better.

3.

Survival of the genetic transport
is easy with all these wrecks
editing out the competition. Almost
a tree of destiny & not random

paintings of pigment crazed with day:
that colour too deep to be chosen
or told, which fades out into the infinity
of explanation. Well almost told.

It is so hard to stand and see it
without mentally saying fir and oak
silhouette. Standing is what it's
all about this nearly blue light.

4.

Inside the matchbox was a library of fortunate records.
Each book opened at the same page. It said
"I am the only survivor". All the rest
now bits of something else. Most of what was thought

isn't here any more. Inside the voice was a timbre
whose emotional colouring repeats in memory for ages
but you can't say what it is. There is no inner
voice. The match exploded and phosphates lit his chin.

He was not burnt. Inside his escape from harm
a child ran trustingly into the floor and cried.
The inside of what is commonly said is larger
than libraries. Bits of else open at the explosion.

5.

Husband encouragement and estimate
die Zeit, signal from my as my
or man city more the twenty nearest
your offshore air so close to oil and life

my weight is down. Recently I have taken
up talking father to father. There are heats,
money changes everything.
The long silences are interesting but pain.

What is underneath here? Do you remember
the act of beginning the process that would end
in its recall? Without point the pencil
still writes. An is between fathers.

6.

Father's eye is large and heard
as ego-I. Father's head is empire
large, or Rushmore hard, father's
word is langue. Men train in the caves

of his chest, and his heart pumps
gravity. Blinking they see TV
lights as they emerge, tanks
face them, they cry staccato bursts.

Father's imago is dead and hairy.
Each hair is checked for signs of life.
One is grass, the next is grass, the next?
Here the scene breaks off abruptly.

7.

Keeping long stations with simplest
daily self attention, hair recalls
the oldest acts of sacrifice, teeth
whiten under the brush of transubstantiation.

Isn't this ritual crush exciting, or is
my hearing clunker mild? Are cats
predestined familiars of banned affection,
or is sitting on the stain angelic?

I really don't think you can use
this imagined tone of meeting
any more. Great leaders flush
with expertise. Say this after me.

8.

Right out of a disaster made
of fire and brush, colored points
line up on the unnumbered plains
with a timepiece's absence noted.

Left to itself the new time is
written over with fallen skies,
bad infinities, sets of red night sun
propose outgoing streaks & worlds,

the way exhibitions stand you
on your own two feet, gawping
as the bits of larger refuse
to be rejoined, on this plane anyway.

9.

Skimboards put in the horizontals
otherwise left to St Malo striped
tops and the shipping horizon.
People beyond counting walk by.

A sea of fronds and memories
easy to second time the colour
of sky and drinks with ritual.
Each entry reaches the same bar.

A hundred grains per second
forming an algorithm of growth,
build up into rock times.
So indistinguishable laughter talks.

10.

Reckless neurone vivacity.
Clear meadows, sheep dip.
Organophosphate amnesia
introduces itself. Strewth.

Am a cop and feel run.
Get or lose. Wiping off.
Précis the euphuism.
Tom the cat. As if.

All there really.
Mitochondria.
Pass by on the other.
Did you read the license?

11.

Strange how the white cloth
backs up into useless memories
for heads down. I can almost
feel the cast of her elbows

round my neck. Not everything
is a blank page, not even
the paper shadowed by the hold
of my watching is all white,

and I wish for less fantasy
to be biding hope, as if it
were a holiday from knowing
where the pillow case blanches.

12.

Wisdom seems to line the carcase
with graspable promises, the sort of
clangs you can pull from shiny unknown
metals, the independence of the senses,

bright colours added to greens & browns,
the shivering cold and shout beyond a wall,
or mementoes pegged up ready for off
on a holiday from knowing, weary

from call-checking memory, you might as well
name feet vehicles. Now there's an idea.
It's gone. If you want more information
call the dictionary helpline. There's time.

13.

Almost ever since your smile
I have known light to bunch
the way paper curls with pressure
and this keeps us working on.

And out of your head. Eyes
ray, nose scents, scanner
morals if your kindness were
cut to hang in folds of love.

Even to speak would house rain,
complicate the era, one sign
and your meter replaces edge.
Just that you're in there enough.

14.

I have almost no words left
for the silent years now the names
have worked with them. Or nouns.
It's as if once was ever's never.

You could help me call in the regress
with attention to my face your eyes'
last dominion, and clique us
while the cathartic expectation toddles.

It's not like that, inhale destruction
the way a smoker, still travelling
outward light of the times,
means this is only my middle word.

Many People Do Not Like The Idea That Time Has A Beginning

(from Stephen Hawking)

Accordance in the reaches of stepping
levels metaphorphised by daylight
over a cup of tea, in morphologies
you wouldn't believe, universalised

as metal exchange ideas. My story
began late but caught up at the turning
as if to report warnings in the ear's
stirrup problematics.

Or this way: the explanation works
like the computer on my desk, connects
the bits of the argument & gets them running
but I provide a content unrecognised

by the machine. Or trip warp your
move. Or believe the next time
on the mandala more than teleological
retroallusions pull branches to the ground.

To the Lifeworld

The validity claim of this parvenu adhocism's
discursive space rackets along the B roads
of a provincial text, or to put it more whitely
the unavoidable insistence of your attributive

greeting is as welcome as smooth sand on a
hot day. It is incredible that this planet
should be one of so many, as incredible
that you will understand this, neurone

different as you are, remember the fast
run to school, that dates you the scooter
the way certain post-adolescent histories are always
contemporaneous, the sincerity exposes wrap.

Or the voice and the legs as "Sir Larry"
put it, the art is detail track to the universal,
or the avant-garde on a give-away offer
between breakthroughs in perception and what

the meaning of this sentence is up to you
but don't delay, history is not on your
side, the piston rings are shot, the day
is expected to be hot and sunny after fog

disperses: the life world disruptions smear
cheese across a pragmatically sense fixed
play world to which the claimant makes
obeisance on old car mats, act your age

be in yourself the zeitgeist at its most
confessional, my hand's sin is not aged
but not young, not performed upon speech,
the language is familiar but the cadence odd.

Forefathers

Swimming in the shrinking gene pool
of my childhood one galaxy could focus
this lion. Underwired hand washable
and very hard to do, we depended
on old varieties decades from now, my

childhood was degenerating corn hunted out
because it has an electric aura for snoopery
outside of its normal lens active zone
of focus. On a cosmological scale who
said your father was lumpy, or ferreting

micro-images, and for fiction? It contains
a museum, some dark & perspectiveless
corners of fear, a superposition the only
thing you have to do on film, and popular.
Its culminating point lies about halfway.

Famous activism, breathless reminiscence
which uncreates those be the last effects
he admires simple. His classics, his
meaningful bristle haircut into the truth
of increments. The past ray of light you.

Romantic Gallery

Seeing through the monument
time stacked shoulder high, wrapped
in lights. This is "my" history.

Conjunction produces nothing.
My silence doesn't mean the world
isn't on. Awareness without names,

yesterday the convenient fiction
of being. Before I knew
these words I felt older than this,

more unimpressed. A few rooms
and a large name heard even
across the world abutted to here.

A sense of the edge, sudden
places and reflexively endless
times merge resistances intact.

Theory 2

This language for government cuts
the signifier off from what the hell
do you think your instantiated nisus

means no word guardianship devolves
onto the inside's intention. How
nice you look in your new arbitrariness

coined in Londinium matted in time
you talk me through it I'll see you
metonymied axial semantic charts

"displode," and if I want to neologise
I shall say what I mean this once, house rules
no abstract pattern of ideal performance

the linguistic archive whispers the new
stories enchantingly on parole from assessment
centres, the word's identity is not binarised

you look so ready to warmly hello or even dance
and I'll address you in code, you'll signify
in ontic questions, and they'll write

theory in three foot high letters of the snows
of yesteryear the ancestors left in the woods
to rub it in, there is no alternative, verbalise well.

Against Interpretation

the insistent generosity of dreams
alto sparkle

and the doing up of recursion that oozes
trapped patterns

wretched citer will you never leave the echoes
an uncertain future

mustily the air tiptoes out of sight behind the bureau
you breathe for pay

so long
the generous insistence of attention surrounds you

Divided by a Common Language

mean modernism is all washed up
so gently in April prose
fiction I don't read any more
wards of what head comic
conjecturology this place seems
prissy text but when I first met
the face of the modern novel he
was a real roving rogue legally
now gathering when an incident
of his infidelity lifts me and whirls
my innocence away just tell him
my name when he calls from the
back door of her home at the end
radical Judson Dance punches me
in the pit of my southwest
of town on an endless stretch
most stores open after a few days
of feeling the moon on all problems
he essentially saw his freshman
year patting the air with yippie
depression retrospective of
films props and masks an art
professional former employee
covers such a function continued
from page man in brain structure
the quantity culture of the corpus
callosum writing about emotions
different neuroanatomists love
this was in brain relations
the event was a student I'm trying
to get at this stuff the media
was having a field origin
of the alleys of daily life
go to work on a poet
closed more by way of feeling

some twenty years earlier a little
depressing to think about bells
I think I can just with what he's
got here the single loss of angry
illusion that language has the
importance it gives S.D.I.
to destroy incoming space
isolated western civilisation
artists will take to the street
world of sleep and its energy
America is to be discovered by
third world countries impounded
by police when indicted on drugs
charges another one who got out
faith in memory and intelligence
spotted the man's car the purpose
of something you feel you feel
his mouth always full of words
jumbo wings and oldies nite-life
Americans for the high frontier
of physical organic feeling
he has to have before he can get
any body bunch tower in the real
run down at a K-Mart parking lot
I look at them a lot I talk to them
I know how old they are their hopes
in public perception at the top
sounds to congratulate art
give off a voice of steely recipience
you can't hear the poetry request
what no man but these true truths
see a guy climb into his mother's lap
conditioning actual persons
function now enlightenment
at the edge of the lips softly we are

not a school now arms apart for the
community read friends or set up
what is meant by a person editor
writing we a mouth's cigarette
made rules for itself on the board
of polished hair and couldn't say
no when offered a performance oh
I wasn't thinking just saving my body
such persons operate in the world
dance just plain catch on hung up
on stone all over the center west
working together in part why that's
something to shoot for the isthmus
of critique's sulphured roar
her associates and I am heartened
there were times we were actually
outside New York all but the
dissertation when I get into the city
I recognise it down a flight of
legendary figurines their brocade
exchange places a syndrome of
nonprofit or to paraphrase funding
sources arts players never under-
estimate adjoining the museum's
broad middle Vietnam war swell
widely applauded for restoring
credibility without scraping varnish
pols reap a year before closing
and becoming active in charities
at what home and homelessness find
when the eighties meet the sixties
the last three and a half years of revelation
have consumed the worst and artists
are invading downtown filler filler
when she involves the cops they

will not be out there looking for it
as a longing on their part I was
always relieved don't think my being
a college sage got it for me it's not
the insurer and the builder you have
street conditions I got the message
less of my mother the book and I
learned to the life in other buys
in violation of the neighborhood
caring for me this single exception
she has two in-house children feet
from the storefront bouncing off
that's in part why I wrote on my
initiative actually today I feel pretty
conservative and on the wall I met
coaxed into speaking questions
if you go back ten levels you claim
"I've never slept with a Republican
of any gender" presenting a point
that has never been fully out
on its own crushes postmodernisn
after performance Whitney craft
stage close as the repeaters for
cumulative burglarised wisdom
wouldn't stay a patrolman for long
or on fire patrol with black arm band
rules I couldn't come back to the U
in this precinct S of A but I don't
see it that way the first girl I let
at seventeen was overwhelming
imagined nuclear flash under the desk
stoned removing all reasons we had
wistful Saturday night specials for
and I had a lot of sex with meeting
and looking out for the negative

that's an easy solution for you who's
forty but I guess that was unrealistic
no matter how far out they are
from your particular politics
after all you read their poems
great moments in the lounge
leading a troop after performances
set up the miniature battle carrier
do come up rainy we pay part of
their tuition the truth was the girl
covering demonstrations dropped
the course a friendly sex life yet it's
really sad that in Philadelphia they
don't all love like the name or grow
up in a small town where everyone
talks cereal and non-verbal justice
had to do something right away after
lying out there for two weeks I had
no mixed feelings throughout the city
crime breaks in and you can't do that
endemic veneer yes no I would say

1989

City Life

Wherever you are, amorous nouns may be at it
all around you, in offices, in sentences, kiosks, colloquia,
we'd hate the kind of conjunction where we just made lexias
on Saturday nights. Oh the suggestibility,
the one hundred index, the customer's always right
even if you haven't bought your text for this year's holiday,
there is still time to look for a deeply scooped ontic rights
    argument,
and the suffering memory videos lent out repeatedly,
or a referentiality special designed for those men
between wool hacking tweed and smarter occasions.

Do you share the ethos of an unblushingly free dialogue
or are you a competitive scream in the city language
of propositional calculus backed by corporate drones?
History threatens to write to the editor quoting the OED
or drop it out of a twin rotor helicopter's grammatical hold.

You might decide not to start reading an experimental novel
in case the hero disembodies about twenty centimetres in front
    of your eyes,
but you'd still be liable to become part of Western Literature
and all its epistemological pretensions.
It is too late, a gang of information technology is breaking in
although you think you're safe rereading Shakespeare's beauty
text suddenly jumps wildly, citations are issued, cognitive grid
    fused.
You see them drop your sentences in surprise and run off,
    leaving you
with a painting: pollarded trees, sand and bathing tents
circa 1890, a story aesthetic tending to the superior wall print.
So many stars in so few years (you know the construction?).

A Bomb's Eye View

astrophysics of an all together now
plunked down, clomp

with gamma cuts and eon waits
is it just to size to be about this big

sorting pictures again (the one scrabbling blood
or could have (betterment or not

the roof is a starting aim
but not to the basement's torn hole

bang you're dead big explanation or sing without pity
connectable hate

on one end a tank's slithering turret and the other
back to school (well they love a god story

it's not any different to go odd and goose destiny
the alphabet is grieving the lost letters

it does help to think cosmos thinks must
have at least a small art

or what then would you do with the spare symbols
if you were to find yourself caught on film defying gravity's
        consumerism

Tell Me About It

"Public relations had passed a milestone on the road to public understanding and respect. It identifies a major interest of the reader with a cause, intensifies his interest and stimulates action. My experience had shown me that immediate results should not be expected, that the impact of ideas is invisible, at first, to the most penetrating eye, and that a time lag exists before an idea makes its fullest impression. We had no concept then of the potentialities of radio, let alone television. The impact of the Dodge Victory Hour convinced me radio was a powerful advertising force. Only one expert foresaw the political impact of radio. And yet within a few years radio was being used extensively to further sound political goals. Experts are effective in evaluating the past, but I would rather have poets evaluate the future."

EDWARD L. BERNAYS, *Biography of an Idea: Memoirs of Public Relations Counsel Edward L. Bernays* (New York: Simon & Schuster, 1965)—extract edited.

The Poetics Of Labour

The government line puts a triple stress
on let's be honest, their mandate,
and new labour. Poetics: my words
have ancient powers. Public
service hotline. Learning to write
the third way, and this from a newspaper
yellowing between the eyes and time.

A minister in the battle of values
makes the white paper charge—
attacks to the left of you, attacks
to the anti-modern (he's called
a control freak). Poetics: free
to choose to work with us,
or, a big or, to hold up your stake.

They say the sneer squad of luvvies
(beacons of hope—call them readers)
will break lines of ordered words
into striking unmanageable demos.
Poetics: join and have your say.
Or is the way that can be told
not the way? Cut. Sim. Tics.

Put Yourself In Their Place

Every moment I would need to refuse
it credence. This couldn't be a policeman
I'm patching together from colour dots.
There is no opening out of this living
room to a world in law. The pretence
of action is not a struggle with injustice.
And I've all but disappeared into society.

One of the uncome plays with a smile
behind the screen-illuminated air.
Entertainment time is entered, taken,
and meant? I worked hard for time,
and now some storying detective
guns down the sound of feeling?
You can almost see a face in the passion.

The never happened calls stridently to me
from across the room with a low rent hum
alternating its sixty cycles with the resonant
announcer giving his deep tone to prince
and drowned alike. Then Nicaragua floods,
Honduras slides into mud, and the telephoto
pulls closer a corpse still wearing shorts.

Another Dispatch

States. Describes. Unwrites. Takes out
of the debate. Entire skullcap. Torn.
[ex] [am] [in] theoretical responses to
what. Remains. Higher authorities. Cruel
theory. Cognitive contusion. "Horrendous"
sight prodding the body with internalized
racism. Outright. Monocausal reasons.

"You didn't have to look for people to kill."
"They were just." There. This point
in the argument lacerates motivation.
The report crawls naked by the grave
officers lubricate with the massacre.
State policy. Is this not an expression?
Increase your knowledge on genocide.

Watch. Like unbelievable. Vividly fire
several shots of the child (here the words
are changed to protect). Lethal rites
beaten with clubs. It's a logical policy.
Take the bodies, divested of points,
out of their containment. Take out
comparisons. Vated [sic] critique.

Escapist Western

A novel with a then and only affect
to mark the lost trail, as if a rereader
had to fall back on the sheer expertise
of history swatting against the backfire.
Hardly anyone knows their horseback,
they can't check the longing, or tame
the usual threats of mountain vision.

It's so past. Flophouse distractions
string you along like the jumped up
pre-modern immigrants making do:
first sight beast sight. Shot
sashaying off to the upper country,
with no aesthetic to speak of, unable
to escape before the acknowledgements.

Like this goddamn fire tower fails
to signal a blaze threatening the senses.
This novel consuming eyes, legs, mouth
of a ranger boy. Remember in slang,
forget with stories the earlier life's
excitable anti-time. It's a feeling I had,
like this is just a story of the west.

Here We Report

Not that this poem seems capable
of irresponsibility, a meteorcriticist
scarring with images of primary impact.
These are lines with a reliable sense
of time, a diagram of fate and other:
the shock of opening, an always changing
middle race, and ambassadorial flare

to close with. You can see for yourself
a dogmatic but chatty narrative, boasts
kept to permeable evidence, weighable
fragments, the sort of re-entry crises
that can be ziplocked at will. And why
not cheer? Speculation is given photo op
subscription paths, fluent rejoinders.

Maybe the impact path is the longed for
vacation, screaming ice to the contrary,
for once its velocity is measured the scale
mysteriously shrinks, the semantic granite
turns out to be cryoconite shrug. But,
and this is a big but, global warming
of the transition melt is less reflexive.

Fire Works

Destroyed by an Air Bomb, an Apollo
Carnival Spray and Colour Cascade,
the Floodlight, the Jack-In-The-Box,
and a Jet Scream. The Master Blaster
lets Mount Vesuvius Fountain, Roman
past candle the shiny shooting star,
a snow storm before the Super Aero-

Sonic Bang traffics in the Yellow Zodiac.
All attention burnt, all sparklers furring
at the bottom of the extinguisher bucket.
Retire immediately. If the work begins
to fire, free the end. Insert to right,
straighten or fuse. Hold onto the torch
and this flowering outburst will heaven.

Lighter of excitement's empire
stand well back from the blast area,
angle away from civilization, the big stick
could land on other heads or houses,
or be lost to the night, or play war
with old Apollo, or even be destroyed
by the Olympian blaster, the star bomb.

Poetry For Dummies

Everything you need to know.
Say the words slower this time,
your plot has been defragged.
To reconstruct the jaw go peer
to peer. Don't let attention
run off and click on the face.
This line explains reflexivity.

You will need to know how
to say that you did not know.
Take your role in your hand.
Identify addressable features.
You may adjust to a higher
resolution, but don't try
the registry. Do this now.

Verify this thought exists.
Confirm that each action
is consonant with the whole.
Do not type anything yet.
Revert to the interface. Run
the known programme.
If a conflict exists exit now.

Finding A Voice

An image of the voice half colored in,
partly interior, partly on to the next event.
A telling example falls silent as I reach
out my hand. Its presence fades
past the sentence. Inside the fact is another
but there's no time to unwrap it.
New social demands take them away.

A voice without a person—how ready
is the culture for it? Do we need spare
persons available to stand by them?
For over a century, the book announced
the end of an epoch where my ancestors
dim the light by which I read by their
headlining. What does this teach us?

Extent, by its very origin, enacts logos
around the known, a sound insulation
for the voice. Amazement at these ends
keeps me away from the argument's jag,
sliding across the smooth impersonals
with my alter pushing from outer self
to articulate mouthfuls of chewy print.

In the Mottram Archive

A collector's afterlife, a tree chant,
an initiation with a free 45,
a tendency not a group, followed
by an advertisement, a reference
to in-the-field discoveries. Smell
of must, not the *community of*
concern beyond this surplus

to requirements library block.
Abandoned fifth, shadowy chairs,
half used third, drab archive boxes
of writing and *tribal poetry*
they say is shared out memory.
Kept texts. One miskey and
the acid free folders are lost.

Bill plays Bach against the dark
(it's *cartoon talk*, thiz 'n then).
Concrete. Structure—does anyone
know what this means, words fall
down the page on an architectural
catenary, missing limbs, phonic hopes
'n no science in memory of all that.

I Left A Little Of Myself Behind In That Novel

How the made is not what you will see
out the window. *I have long suspected it.*
Badness and its injustice of expression.
Post-cryo-revival amnesia. Failure
of will, an in between thought hires
education's arrival spaces. It was me
alright in that novel, my eyes still smart

from what I saw, *biologicals,*
around the cover. No project can
retro-engineer this metaphor into
its safety schedules, there is no sign
how it was made, even the combined
effort of author and *orbital transfer
station* editor leaves the plot outwith

enough to compose excessively intimate
gossip about the anachronistic court
of inner life, civil time and familiars.
On the point of making a prediction
to stop as a new passenger appears
fully dressed, thinking like the hero
to respond emotionally to the culture.

Such Theory Looks Like Advocacy

Taken together, the laminated titles,
the richness of this work, and the soft
cover have not yet said their final word.
Accretion from the contemporary
is in hand. I will leave in suspension
and depart from tradition without
permissible excisions, to imagine

opening the glued sheets, lining
proper editors with ululations
that unfold what I have just called.
Taken with the constant reminders
that after and before follow reading,
the genuine shall then show how,
but let us first recall the machine

that made this book. Labour dower,
bring to mind the commodities to
be signed for, the new economy
designs, parked at the end of a year.
In together's contemporary schools
when the expectations of the theorist
are immense, behind one germane page.

The Unsayable

They say it is otherwise inexpressible,
though only a small *unsayable* secret,
more an order to report back to the wise.
F(x), *F off X*, displays logic and *deus
ex machina* fame. This ever ready
variable, ex of self-expression, ex
of the common voice, is waiting.

A formula in which *thought* is *mental*
and equals the space filled by a body
pressed out of the perforated card.
It's good form. A person touched
only with expectancy. A vapour trail,
a clatter of connectives, a faint *I too*
have nothing to say, no words to say it.

Between nationalism and cult norms
is a longing for simplicity's intention
to elaborate a flowering cliché,
a bug, a warm-blooded inference
surviving on hope. A book of likenesses
speaks to *you* from the unlit shelves.
The heart of the ex plus ex equals.

Blaming The Sixties

To whom this refers. A line of was it
sonneteers for a democratic society
police questioned for those belonging
to groups. The summer of vertigo,
real selves. They say every phrase
can be reversed, they say every
sense made nothing in the head.

Promised to watch the revolution
from the distance of an article.
Scepticism about all the stories.
Sitting on a vinyl floor with the band
dropping acid and refusing to play.
It was still early fall, Nixon was still
president during this harmonica solo.

Out the window a person with really
hot and fluorescent lime style
went on trucking by without looking up.
Oh how can I explain it's so hard to
recount an incident with the unknown
on bass, and whomever on the moog.
An entire epoch in that lost outreach.

New Human Abstract

Dynamic undersampling. Hundreds of trials
(enough to make this true of all humanity).
Detection of class would give culture
a break in the invariance. *Time constant*
in the natural world, *cycles of ambulation*
having a stroll through its beautiful park.
Direction and coherence unite scientists

finding movement in bits that grip onto
one another's pattern. Intuitive appeal
to this *walking algorithm* to be vigilant
in all senses, there's so much flash and hurry
that might fall to *dynamic random noise,*
explaining nothing. These few subjects
chosen to experiment the human race

are proud of their abstraction, their
gait perception, know others are behind
this growing certainty, for a lifetime
of two frames. This predictive undressing
of life on the street might be anonymity's
weapon if the small *point-lit figures*
of self wander at top and bottom.

One

I have simple relations with space
and time. I could not think before
applied observers gave me body
and mind. My clock is always on
and the four sides of myself look out
at the farthest universe (does everything
always have to refer to poetry?).

Once I was really moving,
clock in one hand, gaze in the other.
But I found equations easier.
One is not a relativist at heart,
don't you think? Although
once upon a time I could act
faster than light could show its face,

now kinematic shape is all I have,
and chaos banished. Convergently,
one might think this too personalized,
but without someone to be amazed,
time on its own will mass, poems
hole up, and one is not an imaginary
number, nor waiting to be explained.

The West In Pictures

It drove the frontier forward.
The country shone, thinning out
the light in their eyes. A trapper
stared at print trimming his buckskin.
It's further forward still. Two handed
saw in the cut, arms propping the fir,
ready to fall out of the illustration.

Why go on about this textual scene,
the ragged coat of a man leading
oxen, half the price of mules.
Clean air invented by newsprint,
the ground platforming federal agency.
Plains fell to lard rifles and corn digs.
Brush fire comforts did increase

but the pioneers had a hard social
memory of history as elsewhere,
as far as the eye could seal, then
pulverising it to dust. Norms
arrived by wagon at rush camp
easterners painted into a hasty stop.
Indo-Europeans grew larger.

Deep Time

Biodiversity is a pig if you eat anything,
though not because of the Ordovician
extinction's unmissed clams, and no one
notices Devonian losses, it's the Cretaceous
that trembles the genes. Your body belongs
to them, yet dares talk back to say *skein
of ozone*, as if the genre could handle it.

These corrugated speculations roof
the end of an era, lithograph deposition.
Snout in the fossils I doubt the paleos
have any idea what the will consumes
when millenia work the same line.
Edenic species historicise first,
timed out by *deforestation estimates*.

Pink rounds of protoplasm whirling out
from a tube of gut, straining into formal
dress (*biological drawdown*), staring
across the millenia with a slash and burn
aesthetic. What has evolved into the
truest sentience, left behind as stores
by retreat of the ice. Fossil hunger.

Cognitive Mapping

It may be objected that this following
account leathers partition. Or exists
in a why that cannot be known to us.
Who are we? Who's in a good position
to bank the flywheel of democracy
with advisory zeal and blown particulates
in the air. And why? Gyroscopy?

Theoretically it can swivel, twist, and risk
capital saving justice, but don't just
assume that the landspace can paint,
test that carnelian in a plan of life
whose principles of arrival count.
Have you a licence to practise stucco?
Dissent or no, there's a lot above.

It should be evident that rain doesn't
fall, it is the sky. Money doesn't owe.
Complication is a sea held back by
knowledge. Explain concurrence
as a before and after memory and
money behind the veil of ignorance.
Leather sofa isms. It should be evidence.

Sing Me

Outside vise, reap
honky vision, replay
gravel night. Poets
of lostness
left out of knowing.
Chockwheel insults.
The recipients of

a rehydrated cthonic
slab aesthetic.
Pizzicati wake
of canon thematics.
Smallish presses
national appearances.
Good excerpt recovery.

Umm, umm.
Aleatory pin
metamorphic whizzers
to found poets.
Pass the balaclava.
Ongoing sayso
backs up the analects.

Believe It Or Not

Like the police officer who, in the 1980s,
gradually composed an unidentified
flying object, was later abducted by aliens,
scrapped, and is still not talking.
Why are you telling me this? The pear
ball began to trill rapidly, before rising
up above the mass for 18 years.

Who now won't talk about it. What links
these pieces in my mind is not the large
hovering blocks of light, so generously
unfolding in front of credible witnesses.
Are you telling me this? It's earmarks
lasting throughout an unofficial strike.
Encrypted in the language of minimalism

this spatial craft decides that why you
are telling me can inflate, show, survey,
and mark up, having experienced time
as while the why are you telling me this
fought the overtime constables, an election
which then drifted away high across the
treetops: this telling you, this why me.

Predictive Curves

Had by others now gone
and done, hands running
suggestively over the future.
Instruments of a tamped lust
not this paper nation.
David Blunkett reproving.
A release of energy metaphors,

So solid hon.
Columnar facings,
everywhichway, secret
treasury in—pause—come
based on Humanity's record.
Gordon Brown skimming.
A is mutilating the spine.

In marked contrast.
Cleft explorations, raptured
sensoria, fiscal strip.
Slight foxing in the estimates,
a soft underspend.
Jack Straw being in on it.
A firm proposition.

A Sonnet And A Half For Ted Berrigan

This dude walked into the hall to read
his poetry in the drawer of imaginable
things. I laughed at the cowboy boots'
tactical position. Pressure on the belt
lines flapping. Muting a new theme
I just thought that it was amazing
that one might get to be substantial,

suddenly *to write many many poems*
floral print blossom from endeavour.
Create as morning lights, deconstruct
the twilight, sleep like writing. Fingers
seedy with swoons, clanks of riveted
achievement. Take that cigarette out
of the threat to a technical masterpiece,

and read the whole of a poet on leave
from the army of romantic imagination.
Like a surrealist in a gym, a pastoralist
packing eggs, constitute an imaginary
club and join it. *Somebody is a great*
flying breath *or poems will be lost*
wind giving presence to fragments.

It's A Crime

The intruders, both described as
cool intellectuals, wearing white
male exteriors with excessive pie
in the flesh, left by the fire exit.
Lore: sensitive intelligence seized.
Global capitalism was tucked
under their suits. Unlocked fears

should never be left unattended.
Taking advantage of even short
reveries of the past, modern hackers
steal mobile souls, distracting
the cashier with their money talking
proverbs, like "a pound saved
is a joy forever," or "the pen

is flightier than the cash flow."
Two other youths alarm the credit
mongers with slim, clean shaven
escapes, whilst an accomplice
makes good. Conscience misses
its personal identity in the theft.
Law: meaning follows orders

It Is All Our Story

We are the runaways the paper
wants to find. We ran away with
love and hope, we ran away with crime.
The secrets that live behind our eyes
hide under shades. The Social
want to take us into care again.
They say we run away with much.

At night the colored spots inside
our eyelids flash blue. By day
the court settles its shroud
of propositionality over us.
We ran away to the underworld
of me and you. To prison
unless we give ourselves up today.

We are the runaways the media
catch with ads for pain and loss.
Proceedings have already begun
to return us to state care, yet
we are told by the tabloids to run,
don't let them tell you what to think.
We're all run this way, run that.

Front Line Epic

Arrived at the fifth column of print
to assassinate the memory of white.
You may never be able to read this.
Pyjama prisons, military close-ups
bordering the faxes. Wish tomorrow
to inform you that we will be killed.
A man for each word of the book.

And at a special price (more for each
sentence). Victims know their killers
are colonising them for newsy sacrifice.
Crowd compulsive reading. To buy
lives with UN camp documents of
genocide, I do not sing. You may
never be able to broadcast this fully.

Thermobaric, self-conscious zines
clue into humanity. Gone one eee,
& the final column leaves the place
with understanding in the bag. Type
of singular small deaths. No green
man will say meet mister blade neck.
May be able to read you. Or not.

The Trouble With Metaphors

A public sphere hovered close enough
to see a man's facial hole ventilating
in time with civic rhythms, but sound
couldn't penetrate the bubble, just
light. The noise of dissonant metaphors
for space and tools, birth and building
would have normatively drowned out

a political speech anyway. Common
worlds drove by without indicating.
Morally valuable insights were polite
though one furious life-project lacked
this rational antidote. In trenchcoats
of backward history, critical spaces
gathered outside the originality café.

Categorical imperatives in stylish noir
gawped. As usual, law fed on ethic.
After art I usually go for a long walk
to try and clear my head, but there was
no time to re-orient. Truth employs
big paragraphs, quivering validity
spheres. At least we'd soon be served.

Eat Sleep Work

A world of sweet general relativity
where forty-fives and thirty-three
and a thirds divided commies and fans,
1984 already, and listen, in the hiss
of the future there's a voice singing along.
Is poetry's coping style happy—well?
History in the hand lines, palm up.

Writing cans truth, boxes poignant
anguish, but do we know better?
Sometimes the past is redoable,
meet a friend and rewrite, settle
back after a long and recapitulated
repast. These yearnings flew by jet
from an English airfield with a war

hero living out this time. So it is,
and easy to say that a friendship began
that year, and to await prediction of
cues: sherbert, aniseed, licorice.
Attraction merely a time slide
down n-dimensional long term clusters
of asked-for jobs, networked lyrics.

Based On The Classic Novel

Mrs Lighthouse woke the amorphous bulks
of eyeless impossibility, with life, liberty
and a mirror. This she said, is not you.
The image that was not him blundered
into the line of done moments, one stream
mated itself. Id to base, call me back
at the rock storm. Sleep bolted the event.

Meanwhile you recall this time sopped full
of aftermath waving the gazer to the land.
A natural instinct for explanation decorates
a splendid mind. Each letter is assigned
a poem and combined with many others.
Solitude is the space between the extant
word and the disappeared, a longing

ten years across, sky deep, and moving.
But how true to life? Even if it isn't fine
the sea will be there for this future's
shabby about face. Her family watch him
at her again, she is brushing off the nipple
back into vested discretion, and he knows
she is stocking every second of demon beauty.

Pump-Priming The Economy

Sex born with excrement,
messy sod vitamin
skin for cash, up to the hilt
debut series for the nineties,
poem-cum-perversion
of delayed effect
raised in a cranny of time.

Is is a writer, coyly cult,
an ain't in a go-nowhere
line-out. Taut money,
a jarred centre and grease
beneath the reflexes.
Sweets around the hole
in the caesura flinch.

Gripping from the word.
Written death and sex
reveal force to graffitied
insolent legs. My knob & I
pursue college studies with
fainting biro, ill-used horniness.
Shag fantasy punctuation.

After The DNA Code Was Broken

(for Rachel and Drew)

If only we could find the tone of big science,
and freeze dry twenty one minutes for
experiment's track. Or culture rare sludge
to back going beyond rock's sedimentology.
Rich solution? Make conversation do the work
and house guests those who first imagine
then involve, endearing themselves to the future.

It has an atonal tone, a flirty syntax, a sharp
occulted erudition that paints the poet's gossip
as never again and quiet phones, the A world.
If only we could break into this word.
Modern life forms. Carnal wands. Codons
aren't doable. Classified visions by year and touch.
Now as never before, or nigh as decade,

cities past, cafés of small science,
carried away with the earth's surface.
What about life outside the picture?
Solo meandering as the top down recites life.
Or do we teach deferral to mixing zones
sat in noted tiers for the lecture on passion?
As if we had the science and the chance.

Persuasion

It must always be shown that word magic
is a representation business. Radiate
consumers of assertion, insofar as
making explicit can capitalize
on the past, and make the association
what the audience attributes to the producer.
A common response to think you're free.

Such content. The public interest
was easy to adjust. The operation
of the entitlements to claims could
be inherited. Assertional performance.
Well-dressed men appeared to govern
language use and rational action.
Thought talking to a shadow.

Interpretive equilibrium,
advertising forces, company customs,
repeatable sentential associations.
Are there any *public* relations?
Of status (this is philosophy), authentic
luggage (this is publicity), the game
of conclusions (this is the account presented here).

The Eagle Book Of Imperial Poetry

To write a poem to?
Scenes with life-like
imperial tint.
Never is now on the map.
Poem writes in blue
without a colour word in sight.
I.T. of empire eg. irreal

That's my Aleph,
you are meant to say,
defends the land of hope
and finale. Place
leaving is done, doing
is anticipation. A poem—
from o to ∞.

Viewless mathematical
symbols? Mountains
rise, land forgets
to write the poem.
Was in the blue pictures.
Or then. A then. Poem
of thens and will be's.

That Turner Prize Bed
Turner Prize Show, Tate Gallery, 1999

With a classy degree in find art
and aborshun, she is painterr
NO MORE. "I gave up Art
compleetly in 1991."
Righting been explore a shun
of the sole concept
to dysplay pillow talkie.

Hole psyche of whoman
life, totalic new medea work.
The next room's reel makes
uz look from new perspextiffs,
an eve owes complex eemoshuns.
Partickle bored effects
"Working in black and wide . . .

without distractshun of collar."
Words get down to laundromat.
Rose of unmanslot mashjeans.
The twins have a bodying poor
and foebeers. Memory thinks
to reveil in there arty fission
they conshushly borrow from 99.

Some Syllables Are Missing in this Elegy

Home with just erosity, honour
darting among the ies in the closet
where each passion is classified:
mium, heliotrope, carmine.
In on the world again, utopian
pasts tambourine. Day silence,
night silence, sitting headiness.

Why did I leave? he asks you.
Message from the dead party
opens the letter suddenly a friend
talking yore again, one who
knows what you're thinking,
pills and lineage, all the frizz.
Yours? Fuck-off rhymes, sand

in the worlds one lives. To lose
the community of spectres and still go
ward. His gangly inner voice will never
graduate from hallucination
with others, fly out of plat shirts
with a corporeal look. Have confidence
in the won munity. Put on the com.

The Personal Poem

Lying flat, I was loaded head first
into the MRI scanner, a launch tube
to eternity, and each of my hydrogen atoms
flicked its dipoles back and forth.
My brain was palped by electric fields
patterned to a Steve Reich rhythm.
White scientists in a periscope controlled me.

Thought is a measurable field of fat
and magnetism. The fat remembered
then let the atoms of inner thought
fall back relaxed into non-alignment.
I is an invariant element to this physics.
Forms for consciousness and stop
all too measurably afterimages.

High pitches enter the right ear
and cross through the perilymph
in search of an audience. I register
the fairing scored with manufacture.
Opening sounds hash, *informe.*
Channel panic. Each sound is a hit.
Each word of this anachronism it.

Time Team

This is day one and already we have cinctured
rapacity, made a few finds and now the death
of classicism has stopped escrow. Mind you,
the designers have already planed the timber
and the trench across the hypocaust pleads
for brawn. It's a dilemma, and the records
of sponsors look worse than the geo-poetics.

Maybe three days is not really sufficient life
for a novelty. Even the screen has advertising
in the wings. Measured across the I told you so
with the force of many hit shows, and the
nostalgia of a decade of last nights, the past
exits. Dinosaur outfits on the left, hominid
shell suits to the right, souls up on the shelf.

How would they have used this engram?
Our reconstruction shows the granite buck
as it might have looked at you from a moral
valley, or anyone with attained beliefs.
Now it is the last day, and the discoveries
of gender, class and former sufferings
have been cleared up. Next week the future.

Cinematics Of Memory

No dream, as in you are not there, can incline
lives I am always already to rough cut.
When it's over I leave, the close-up glows
with a cigarette shining hairs on the nude back.
In living there are always curves to remembrance.
Every frame shows the city rusting on wind
and gone, day rents night from a metaphysics

only the truly shocked eyes can cordon.
Epic is history's souvenir menu, the sweet
memoried lyric a stain of chocolate sourced
in poverty wages. Hasty repercussions
back to the wardrobe. "The body is too light,"
says the director. "Is that what the dolly shot missed?"
Face in need of cherished imagos.

The *auteur*'s daily confession, the one
in the scene, thumb over the lens.
What else can a post-aesthetic eye do with beauty?
City smarts, and oh what a sundered life,
the next moment the music stops, steps
echo with imminent copyright, a leg
vectors across the screen. Time has been had.

Paternalisms

1.

Language's strong need to be loved, salaried fight
to stay adequate to that ripe, gorgeous reality
whatever it is, that unfolds directly, full
of conflicting urges and symbols, authentic
within its selfish rebellion from the chains of
syllabary, aloft in the ferris wheel of archaic
pictograms which leave us wanting more.

Augustine once said "Talk some nonsense"
to move his frenzy kiln wards, just living
the integrity of domain. His working
is different now, he waits for the words to come
to him. His nonsense is well finished.
Refers his fluency to a haunt, and poetry
the snicket at night, cycling fast without touching.

Representative of the object world, his child,
nature, glyphs, adequate dad's word
is alleged to be an upright presence
hot from the struggle at the crossroads
where the signs said Thebes and Truth.
Later his utterances act out the future
thinking it's the past. Phone the Hopi.

As I speak, father is made present.
He is what permits the air between us
to resonate its cavities with hearing and telling.
He is talked into existence, the play acted
by the voices of all his people. He is made
the universe of discourse, and billows forth.
He is the analytic father, phallus in mathesis.

Or so these men say. A large raindrop
on stone paving is clear through despite
the always already swirling oils on the meniscus.
These men's books are the whole of language.
Inside, the dead fathers try to find out
what is going on, the larynx is out,
the fax down, they think a woman would help.

"He did not know that he was dead" wrote Freud
describing a dream. Years passed and no-one
did the obvious, insist on an answer
to their question, what did he need?
No one. Not that nothing happened there.
Ghostly meals were eaten. He thought he thought.
And still the narrative was binned.

Shiftings and the varying true marked him
from this time. Idle, later his psychological
object was a piece of compacted apple
rejecta from a child of his. Later still
a feeling of being became more English,
as if the former allotment still grew to
the low end of the plantains in subscript.

2.

You've seen what they can do, these supermen
at the court of Romanticism, Survivalists
without origin, scraping hard skin with pumice,
working out to avoid productive labour
as they gaze into the eyes of the opposing grunt;
a sharpened bayonet as being for world in advance,
obscures the loin cloth of street cred reason.

Crude imitations of the poetic sublime, secret
almost to say means he had thought this
for a long time in the sixties, this extended
life line chaos wholly undetermined violence.
"Ours is the best effort to get out of the twentieth century".
Arise condition subjectivity, show the assemblage
of current mentation cargo cult and offshore.

That was when his century was twentyish plus
his hair was believed by the regrouping cops,
suddenly punching, dragging plainclothesmen,
he pulls out an empty Seven-up can, symbolic issue,
and flags for a real down; bad vibrations
the system increases with pressure according to
fairly simple relations. Like—evidential.

A literate enzyme he, cellular access course
to Derridoid, all testosterone and 5 point answers
in conference debates. His clothes murmur
of seamstresses in Taiwan, his words are read
off what he calls discourses, and he laughs,
rubbing his forehead, sittlichkeit's my last word
on the subject, see, people, through the windscreen.

I'm always in a dark space when I'm a man.
He motioned to the deflagration on the street.
A bus changed gear. List the unimpacted areas
and when only occurs to explosion depend on it,
they are confined. Yes, I am a man's dark
build up of shock front. Neat. I'll
give it a go. Not suprising mass, not ignited.

Feminist men simultaneously set in
track position relays, blunder panels,
speaking for you and me into dialogue
with emery confessional techniques heating
the how-to mandates. Let's face it,
the general is pulped. On the other line
now, difference is awaiting issue.

I am converted so often now the spin
of new conviction is necessary to keep plans
ready for veggies and those heavy breads they sell
at the wholefood. It's hard to find the words
for this and let the painful counterfoil
rip out the language's metropolitan buzz,
to where out in the shadow lands time was taken.

3.

We've stopped counting them. We have
attempted to withdraw all our abusive
languages. We have managed the our
self less well than our mandate committed
us to. We are still talking but some
silences are settling in. Please listen for
further. There are still men to be found.

Meaning that when we return from our tour
of the defences, our uniforms appear out
of place, and when we speak, people
no longer understand our simplest references
to the war. He talks about his grandfather
who now lives in another place. Later
he seems only words, authentic enough, but words.

In the drifts of recorded music his thought
was stitched to the inexpressible, in writings
he could talk to those with just the one answer,
in his soi-disant imaginative space constant
troop movements of ideas and memories gave him
a sense of power, in time he could tell
there were stories repeated in scholarship's eye.

That hedge is here or ruled over or
come back and infiltrate my affections with
extremity. Its limit is where we've been
able to cultivate up to, hands short and my son
away at the front. And I work best
when there is too much to do. He listened
to people stabilise the emptiness of detail.

Others chose him for their team and made him
a silent majority for political battles while he
slept and worked as appropriate, loved and ate
of his own volition, believed possibles, drove
hard and was found half eaten by rodents
in a thicket north of here. His vehicle crashed
he was beyond recognition, but male definitely male.

Ultra sound showed calcification of the will
to aggregate piecework, his septem wall
screamed with pain jamming a wide sayable band
dismembered groin catheter reach fed
inside the chambers of his Id, this once
employable body now flushed out into the writings.
Reception is not possible love, not working.

Masculine products of decomposition luminesce
then back off the detonation zone, faltering
in their steel cage cars, history's overhead
charged the men with initiation. Tribochemical
features used to back form the continuum
of explosive affect followed by deadened response.
Hardness particulates the aesthetic manifestation.

4.

Young pilots with export mentality, haptic
brilliance, and market vigour, flew the imperium
craft, sub and hyper space. Unsuccessful
regional ventures began to diffuse their horror
stories throughout occupied space. Classic
early adopters seemed to lose blip when disparate
points in the galactic limen syzgyed for reasons unknown.

Paternal loss making surrogate chip set
dream blank, dancing, hiding one's hands
under the stiff cape of a white surplice.
Your father looks in your eyes and sees
his own gaze back at him. Silence compacts
to localised nodal pressures as the bathysphere
descends his memory. Each wish has found a niche there.

Our young hero was lucky. Purely rational
trialability, affect warehousing, plus
interrelated order distantiation, left him
on his own when the ship's breakdown occurred,
prior in this rare case, to entering hyperspace.
The other crew were friendly but older men,
interested only in discussing boring stuff

like the merits of pre & post natal cognitive programming.
During the months they were stranded in that sector
the pilot began to wonder why the imperium
failed to consider the distributive entirety.
It was rumoured that all space drives were built
outside known space, beyond this happenstance.
He was bored. He read the small ship's library.

The obvious identity of gothic spire, rocket
and erect member calls us into an age
actually in parallax to what gently severed
iconologists call our own, as if detained
under a sort of Prevention of Terrorism act.
Age to will in experienced callings
to the body to answer: just a word or two.

Then he discovered an archive in the cargo.
Called residual externality in symbolic domains
it covered mostly ancient history and expansion
records. Body axis precessed over a new eidetic
range. He left the pilot service on his return.
and entered university. Superordinate factors,
crossmodal plans from the imperium were not evident.

No one could call the crossweave of basal
scholarship adamic, but in his role as president
federal accidentalism was seen from time,
enrolled scribes gave him popular station
segregationalists of readership could not refute.
His speech was challenged singularity.
No signifiers where he came from, none expected.

5.

A kid out of modern subjectivity, this
chunky thighed historical man plays Cupid
conqueror to the achievement of humanism.
The skin shines, the slightly rounded plateaus
of muscle shadow abdominal creases, and it
resembles historical relativism but grins cheekily,
as if say Caravaggio were a lover of such events.

When I'm grown up I won't need you Daddy
or to mime your yoga headstand on the armchair,
don't want to, don't want to, can't sleep.
Looking up from paschimottanasana, then again,
his father's startled, the boy looked man
when the west side, the back, was stretched.
Adam crater nob and pitch future throw.

Paternal words collected and burned, or
deposited under an information act until
above the memory barrier instantiation hits.
He emerged as an instruction. Given over
to physical support the state and action.
Soon there were only set standard nomenclatures
riff high on the patrilocal holding zone.

His first memory is a doorstep. From there
he climbed into what later gave space
and monumentality. Pointed to the dread
men were showing one another but was told
that could not be said in language, not
even the showing everything has. Given books
a whole way of being for himself opened out.

Third, manly inductance over older distances
wound on a core of competitive language games
depends on the magnitude of limb manipulation
surging phonetics, and remember how handsome
it can look due to the hysteresis effects.
Conjugal dyad flashburned onto the wall
spreadeagle site of the body's fall by I left.

Ordinary communal events don't need to be
hardened in lucite, famous mark words,
a new kickstart within the welded
frame of the old pragmatic verbal futurity.
And there he paused. His oratorical idiom
could be heard faintly under the hiss, coerced
gently into the audible by the amplifier's interpretation.

Hands: for folding around and squeezing
the steel framework built to resist, no
stroke use of skin receptor texture here.
Shoulders: measure arm's throw by curve
rested on the bone shelf, burdening clavicle.
Some work where they can't fuck with your mind.
Off limit field body potential gunned.

6.

One imagines, you suppose, they infer, I know
the problem is invention, the suprised idea
that persuades slowly like a warm room when invisible
cold patterns collapse, wriggles clump underneath
one's surface, your skin, their world, my proof
of limitlessness. Then its lack of conclusion
becomes the only greeting possible. By what right?

Memory carries across the bridge of disappearances
some continuity, wrecked paper, the permanence gone,
there was never now one, and the control of pasts
sees my hand is still the same one you saw before.
Piling up the precious onto this rapidly filling moment
crammed with dead signs and heaped minutes stacked
over the years in an uninterpretable this.

In my picture you are always entering the room
just before you discover the eradicator moment
and stop talking to us. You stay there outside
hoping one of us futures will walk round the side,
take your hand, and say something about the benefits
of this loss, so you can dismiss us to everland,
and we stay hiding back there, watching you mind.

My though seems to be thought, what was I thinking
just now, then, before this, how can I go back
and check, I want to know what it was really like,
not some similitude, some art stuff protected with
iron and rhyme. This was very frightening, then,
but now it is already a long time ago, go through
it all again will make the more the after asking.

Eventually will not eventuate, you will be listening
to another line of music, the corsair will be unmasked
to say a few words over the pyre of his friend's poet,
to tell the sinking story over and over, differently
so that he could go on planning to get it right.
The story refused. The music refuses to stop now
and its words are in no language I ever heard.

This is not an economy of credit or signs but memes,
the coins of past rated at a standard unit of recovery
taking control of the atomic structures, this here meme
will stop him going into that store and arriving at the till
without produce, put that meme in writing, and this act
is part of the fix. Dance economies are always over,
and a one and a two and a swing your self up and over.

The bones, the thoughts, the nothing explains such unknowns.
The beauty of flatworms a pattern voided by the lines
of the letters. What is not to be said is said
in the face of reckless delayering. Blunt and nicety.
Come out from under the net and sing a few words
midsong, go through the entire memory without much tune,
hearing backwards, one confrontation at a time.

7.

Good stratigraphic physiognomy,
some buried sleet in the occipital,
ice masses with a spinal corridor
south into the seminal vesicle.
Chipped extinct bone fragments
of those times we, you know, sort
of got it on together. Some fluting.

Styled carpetbagger. Energy as cliché,
ensemble raddle, entering the shelter
that expression preserved in rock fall
by submergence and sand burial, rocks
open a new heartening. The northern
peoples see no land beneath their feet.
Spaceships open new fictions, variegate, die.

Razed, your several bodies merge into
one corpse. Raised with an S you
exonerate everything. What's underneath
the path, he asks. Earth. Why
is it earth? I can do standing up wee.
Rays of dusty sunlight move him to tears.
The stereo picks up CB radio. Hyphen spite.

No man. Utter heresy. Crimp knuckles.
Fire line. Alto sax. Me source.
And then the mist withdraws into fine points
revealing not the being but ship timber
charcoal in sand. Some rashes last
years, decades to know your skin,
as wheel invents the human and circles.

So hasn't one, changed nature
though we may have, definitively
the call wrong in our doing so,
bound together by earth and seeing,
a belief the others did infer roundness,
long before you were born, we trust,
but not that they were making a mistake.

Estimation free, unweeded hair,
more men than ever constructing
want reign packet radio hard thermal
vest. I understand your concern,
my dad wouldn't like it either,
he'd go ape if I, he knew, but
coin rich avenue baste, epithalamion.

You must stop talking to my dreams. I find them
weeping in corners of the town, or renting garages
and pinning up murder stories from smudged tabloids,
or finishing PhDs on the habits of phenomenologists.
They shrivel into carboniferous esters, sort burn
edged reps, they don't represent the telephone
or the theatre. You must stop taking the dreams.

8.

Finite skies over the marram grass closing the set.
He has arrived from the north with travelled shoes
saying, is this supposed to be a way station,
this house of many sounds, I checked the extant,
don't leave me merely depth making existences
aesthetic futures. Here, have my coat, put it over
the naked light, those photons were mine once.

Hysteria it isn't. Not coming out of the shiver,
that's the next one, the coming line of time
that the shiver is in for, whatever started it
has escaped. If only I could add to the past
a little of the present's addition it wouldn't
miss it would it, could it, help it, stop it.
When the circuit reflexively affects the current.

Trade has climbed up this hill from the deep water
in tiered houses, the sugar was so desirable
they could almost hear the cars queuing to eat,
and the distance is no object applied to time
I reckon a Platonist always expects to find answers
waiting outside. It's not the time, it's my hand.
Some times are separate from the moving limb, no?

Have you been talking to the future again,
engaging its bidding look with explanations?
From here I can see what was once a field
and once an upland wood, rupture into housing
insides. Are you an inside too? Can listen
moralise with its canny knowledge of outcomes?
Now what past are you forward of this time?

Expel, cloaca man, desert tumps up your lost bit
looking right at you as if you were the ghost, titrate
of reasons, daylights and systems, is the finality, dream
reaching a velocity which is end gulfed, swallow led.
Morality is quantumised symmetry breaking, so should you
remember the friend stealing you, push hard, thin paper
will be enough, enough on the land that is all remains.

You debrief his phone part nature fascinated
by its apolitical hold on the back of the neck,
sweeping in front of a waterfall. Come and look
at economic suffering's on screen flicker if you want
to see what we do do. Hey check out that collage.
what a laugh, grille, fumbles camera, waves
round the green smoke in the video clip.

Uncurl and arch your years in the irremediable line
of analysis, the sky is spilling over, warm winter mulch
is so English, rotting down pears and grass, laurel
and the war was wearing silkscreen, marching on
rollback, nostalgia the clear and present danger.
the word several lines back was too quickly over for
what was wanted. Try asking, or free the associate.

9.

Presuppose a radical critique. Harp
on it, play the line out beyond hope
to triangulate the sympatico regularities.
Oh me, oh my, we are interspersed
with members of the opposite, sigla
rules, you know it makes sense
precipitate in hard but distant clear surfaces.

Say out of it again, meaning a
behind the seeings preconceptual
touch that makes clay just clamp
the armature as the time is soon
over with, north of where you recall
as now so much said is a cornered
whisper to the gods, if the stalls hear.

Made his way to the emperor's consent
and while recovering from melancholy
any existing illusion witness to his life
hits the badly drawn monster with a kick
learnt in high school martial arts classes.
Though he never became a modernist
his life was one of exemplary virtue.

Mystery conglobed charitable action
at the lengthening day's missing end
he ran the expectation through again,
hating himself, Aloysius to Ivan,
plot hell, scream at his attack,
go out the window, read the leader,
fantasy murder the prime minister.

We gradual as police charges and then bursts
of sincerity, we serious blobs of concrete
young shields of digression are wise
to their communication, we dance
speeds of attention, disengaged red
streamers out in the corner of the eyeball.
What I am now going to call us.

Making theoretical insight noises we rushed them
past police guarding these passages jumped out at me
I couldn't tell words spread. The bottle of self pity
in observation of the arse to tail I could identify
anything that revolution. No really, the
anaclitic was out on the street, strutting
its new power, interstitial history.

Mob of claims for auscultation, sit down,
your threads are bare, babbling incoherent
but move me, an I contained in the square
live feedback. Claims on the state will be paid.
The going rate against my goals and I have seen
Downing Street emerge with a metaphysic of passsing,
and I advise myself to run, out, out or miscall?

10.

In ever seen pellucid green rendered
a growing up sliver of a me gone
to an old illumination in crystalline
rambunctious prayer. He stands astride
his charger, the battlements lay the base
line to a grass colour you could sustain
yourself with, in the gilt, from most, small.

Manhood has a speed, event time
radiating from the polished gesture of bone
moulded with facial padding, the
jaw is wired for the command line,
monitoring thoughts as the mirror gradually
unsilvers shred by chert. He says love
and means only that act, word and it.

Argue with say. Argue with bad.
And the was it. I can see your need
wiring your jaw for a straight smile.
I see your hope gets you through
the next hour. But by what measure.
A tip of convolvulus shoot seems so still
as it grows furiously; so green, so hopeful.

Are all thoughts memories? Which
memories of age eleven are aches
deep in the shin bone? Why this
insistent speculation? Is it a refuge
this argument about conversation running
my head? From what flattening impact
of usual townscape, irregular pavement?

Isn't it a bit late to get talk to mean let alone
to catch history by guessing lucky? My shirt
protects me from chest colds, my shoes
from hookworms, my trousers from lust's
death and my jacket? Do you know what I just said?
Something with plenty of pockets (feminine symbol)
and maybe not too tweedy (of mixed but strong fibre).

From torn out limbs knowledge, that person
is my penis, not some phallus, restore it at once.
Lessen the silence with conversions.
Give me your hand. The lines I will
read in a moment, but first, the plumped
abraded skin; that is a reading. In
your head you're shouting, out here, tranquil.

Oh yes, he walked up & down lengthways
for years, a hand waving to just miss
doorjambs and breasts. Muddle through
the power and metaphysics if you must but
no more alliteration, it undercuts your
semantic intent. Oh you fool, you've lost
your key, read a master, try to represent well.

Next Gen

"Yet what must be explained on the Melanesian side is people's simultaneous construction of Europeans as spirits and their nonchalant acceptance of what Europeans regarded as technological marvels . . . One might suppose it was the Melanesians who had a sense of power. If the advent were treated as a performance, akin to that of the masked dancer, then who was the producer of it? . . . My guess is that an initial component of people's terror may well have been at their own power—at what they had done to bring about an enactment of a quite extraordinary kind."

MARILYN STRATHERN, "ARTEFACTS OF HISTORY", 31–32.

1/Civil society

And you ask me what I mean by polity
How can I answer, you cannot touch it
They didn't do that plunge very well
Exhaust billows stir up bits of visibility
Most of the moral world is not present
to the dressed eye, though to bare belief
the seen is tattooed with implication
Perhaps I should use the edified style
Dim forms in cars—are they saying
to themselves, I am a chip off society
How many can fit into one dream
Take the unseen clouds up in the sky
out over the sea, they suddenly loom
modern and scientific in polarised light

Such downbeat odic pastoral
is one portal users go regardless
to wring committed performances
in great heaves of flayed musculature
and spiritual geography's loose flowers
as short shrift poetry wings
and joints the skylark

We're not big vacation people
No matter where you go in the world of cardinal virtues
you want to come home at the weekend to a poem
that as Sean O'Brien reminds us is a "place"
where "paraphraseable meaning has been drawn"
Now that's a good feeling

2/Lyric moments

I'm wearing a bracelet of self-counting numbers
    which rise to two hundred forty thousand
    then begin again without stop, tick, or judgement.
Not some new gadget which counts erect seconds of a life
    without the eternal return.
Innumerability is waiting everywhere, so I'm glad to be attuned
    to all my co-timers.

One out of many in a worried stumble from sleep's temporal
    silence
I run to hold my hope sick child who's folded into an armchair
She holds a yellow swirl a potty returning light vomit again.
Television is singing the stardom of Notting Hill to her
while Lyn Hejinian's diary whispers The Cell's
perceptual confession into my coping strategy
to pass as language throughout my head.
Does my racing heart beat to break or rejoin time
I'll pass on that.

3/Political subjects

A prime minister would be an indivisible person
even inviting the porn webmaster to tea
but which cortex of social capital should pour
Evening lights make varying distances thinkable
though an unidentified orange glow in the mist
might be no fire wall just an enlarged streetlamp
George W Bush's facial expressions flicker uneasily
as they line up with divisions across the continent

The party wants to see modernity risk boom
The country regrets Amritsar, the Belgrano
global warmth, the regret is visually beautiful
in which prosperity and opportunity glow
The community is talking about a vague man
a sulky man a man who holds us together
Of benefit and work, spires of insular justice
Reflectively colored transportation surfaces
and not one single epistemology in sight
We will also continue to tackle failure

4/Drives

auto wheels levered in the palm
how clever the small shifts in life

moving fast enough for anonymity
eyelit pairs sweep the culture

a noun for vector persons
to feel a feeling is not allowed to happen

transnational minims
stuck between fields of small vegetation

the self a small button
another dissolves in holding networks

an unemployed European conflict
listening for the air's gusty arrival

intravenous digimania
white waft oriented retail

radio music perjures regret
to justify itself says the phone

is this the Fall this singularity
transmitting body to home

head for the underworld
definite article in the past

a tunnel sprays connection over and above
whether to shake or hug on arrival

5/The new anthropology

One evening I was watering the garden
in that southern city when a canvasser
of that time and place stopped to ask
Are you a subject of New Labour
are you happy with this attempt
to measure the emotional literacy
of institutions, is your ethnography
enabling the creative civic powers
Before I could answer a single mother
walked by and he blushed then tried
to explain that it was her witchcraft
a snake in her vagina strangling him
Later in my fieldwork she explained
his hatred as a pact with the devil
He transfers money across the world
and yet fails to help his own relatives
In the months that followed I devoted
considerable gym to these questions
Anonymity of world as weight and pull
Watching four channels in one lifetime
the body mates with the pedals and levers
for fifteen minutes of Kilroy empathising
And a man is being beaten on screen two

As we docked my poet friend met me with a story
of early morning subjects in the country of Marvell
Here even a dog turd on the shingle is civic indifference
I noted crowds shopping for the continuity of showing forth
Their modern market likes the politics of the belly
In convivial lagoon hangouts time is a blue flume
Stretched on a thin pole the bicycle bodies worked
past as I asked the poet if modernity's waterpot
fertilises the garden with its willing magnetic dots

6/They bring us words for our poetry

My people who wait for inventions
to give names to parts of their flesh
and memory they never had before
Open fields of email twenty four hours
A hunk of philosophy still hangs about
the new technology and its sex keeps
the hello screen friend expectant
When you are always online people
attempt to scan you for vulnerabilities

My language is a set of search terms.
The collective narcissism sees its beauty
given back by the information stream
stripped down to a few typable words
My sex hands immanence on to flesh
A thigh becomes a position in space
it creates and edits cell positions
with just a small shock of profundity

My relations are buyable technologies
One sends an attachment to the public
square screen in mobile phonetics
stored in the west where each listing
is a torn strip from an unknown life
none of those listed as Hugh Philips
(the smoker, doctor, meteorologist)
are the man I went to school with

My own narrative? Begins with wartime
codebreaking, suddenly rationing stops
fighting secretly to buy goods at the mall
Is this language now less intersubjective
Interrupting packet voices don't answer
Yet it's been a good day the rain held off
air was clear roads consumed the spectacle

7/Beyond Vision

There's no "sex" in Buffy only sex
Demons ariels and vampires
attack its skin and tone with acnes
of fear, because here everything
is sexualised eversion
of erotic zones
from the underbody
of new desire.

In these daily teratoid dramas
skin is it, and the two body
problem of smooth visibility
in one unblemished zone
is so so ordinary
its primetime fate
is up in the air

The slayer is usually right.
"Yeah" says the tomb demon,
" I had a sadly intense temper"
Then he's faded to the next day
and it's back to school again.

8/Dogs, Dragons and Tygers

I am trying to connect the macaw to the dog
who is in flight to the moving train to what
cannot all be in the same spotted afterward.
A perfect eyebrow moves into position
just a second too late for the emotion.
Don't you just love to go up the eyebeam
and into the large beckoning arrangements
of onscreen cause and effect. I know I do.
Just one more world for a crowded brain.
Don't you dare to read a politics of white
and black ethics of the mean as an aesthetics
of bourgeois acceptance into these dalmatians.

Parents enforce obedience to the plot
(they are plot) to be watching is to have
a left and a right and this is inescapable.
No mobiles, no television, no gravity
in this roof running leisure world.
Perched on adjacent flapping trees
they can test each other's swordplay
and we all know what that means.
Not wishing to be in their arms
the warrior monk says he is nothing
all things are nothing and meditation
brings a white place of endless sorrow.
At twenty five wisdom seemed formulable
a deconstruction without professionalism.
So she literally dives into the miss
(should this be mist and how we can be
up so close to her and stay up is unclear).

9/Online enchantments

I should explain that in this game I am a mage, this spell
    temporarily reduces
the other's intelligence in this world reclaimed slurry of cultural
    memory
How they died our grandparents curled around the last day in
    their cots
Hopeful symbolic elevations of decorated facades lie above the
    chain stores
I had already forgotten the invasion and its marble
    achievements
though my memory still fingered a cramp sometimes while I
    slept

If you can accept that these tiny moving symbols are persons
the second half of this life might well be positioned globally
and who knows I may be able to copy it on one of the children's
Hi everyone it's me says the blocky purple figure (who is me)
Remember that people on deck can be damaged normally
and roads will move with you in their accelerated perspectives

Remember that your skills deteriorate at a much faster rate
    while you're dead
I do believe we must resist this mild epidemic grief because the
    if only
is a dear rain and like the rest of this country I love its offspring
    too much
especially in the mood that stares at photos of old friends when
    they were thirty
Now remove ignore, remove receive, grant speaking privileges,
    optimise lives
And as for reference well I just don't do business dinners for
    anyone

10/The Sonnet

Did the Russian philosopher really
smoke his manuscript
Is it likely the text was never written
the supposed destruction of two copies an alibi

With no institutional backing
just the moral integrity of assertion
The angel of formalism wrestles
with the angel of sociology

A tone of scholarly surprise at error
is highly effective
Winter afternoon light attenuates the blue
I stare into this sun without filters

Temporary meaning will have to be enough
Smoke that gets in your eyes

11/Poet and critic

Do I know what Denise Riley means by the "partly"
when she admits to a feeling of guilt
"partly generated" by language?
What does Wayne Booth mean by "trying"
when he assures us that "in a month of reading
I can try out more lives than I can test in a lifetime?"
Maybe "the problem we have to discuss today is beauty"
as Isobel Armstrong's "Beautiful Soul" replies
to a critical "Benjamin Reader" of Adorno?
But I so much want to believe that the poem's halo
really is greedy in a rationally defensible sense,
that the fault in creation is more than a lost god's scripted rift
in J.H. Prynne's peripatetic poem "How Many There Are: A
       Letter"
whose pages are curved models of a lost term ethical treatment.
And "As I walk down the fold . . . the progress of relevance"
is explained by a linguist friend returning from the school gate
as the career of Gricean implicature into relevance theory.
One tends, says a reviewer, "to hear beneath it all,
a rather charming, approachable voice"
In this series of faintly intoxicating thoughts is each term
a simple function of its position whose sum tends to one?
Argument requires local stabilities of reference, form progress
limbs lift and modern urban structures to channel the
       reviewer's
"movement of meanings" well out of sight in sanitary conduits.
I would like to blame this confusion on the reader who is
       listening
to the quiet internal rushing of some anti-depressant the
       manufacturer
claims "sedates yet promotes activity" but this too may just be
       sediment.

12/The body

Angry muscles clamp the head's pipeline making the pain shift
    restlessly in its seat back of the skull
But where has the aching, expectant plot gone
If I talk too much the doctor will hear a parodic self-diagnosis

Waiting for a chest X-ray I read the Tinnitus Quarterly and
    learned that when the noises are really bad chewing gum
    helps
And the volume often varies after lying
Dark wings of lung in the photo turned out to belong to the
    man before me

Emotionally insecure media promote answering anxiety attacks
To me, says one letter writer, snoring related hair cell damage
    could provide a plausible explanation
Avital Ronnell, however, says "the only possible ethical position
    is 'I am stupid before the other'"

Wires to the head and wires to the wall and wires to the would
    be society
Sound without memory of sign goes straight through the bone
    to widescreen soft tissue
Does it con the neck, react in the brain lab, and enter thought's
    conduit that way

Nomad pain is the not-not-I
A moving planar curve creating new forms of anguish
Architectural, a romanesque occipital dome whose interior is
    stripped to a dingy whitewash

Often the cure is to take the patient back to the mother moment
    the lover's car
Certain of the conditions exercising heads include dulling,
    coring, and gnostic engineering
Align require and design or writing may run out of song

Unbelieving chores broken prayers justified consumption
And then I heard simplify, simplify and now everything else I let
    slip
Do you know the wireless application protocol for this induction

I was utterly and totally stressed says the singer in my head
Barbara Kruger matches aphorisms to state moods
My own irony id quotes a website saying, we are always
    connected

Cures line the plot with a Cistercian white, a lover's gum, a
    completed ache
Wires transmit I feel your pain
Into this what shall I call it still ringing sociably in your ears

Expressions

Californium 98

You cd get too smart says the agent
if it wasn't the chink the fruit the Man
the hour when a guy can't stay honest if he wants to
have a Manhattan poolside at the cocktail hour
the block looking just as it had looked the day before
hard solid concrete around carbon rods to absorb
neutron bullets, strange particles
"I have a loud gun but it doesn't have to go off"
a bum scene and a bullet punctures his chest
with a handkerchief & lifted my gun
using the nucleus of Uranium as a target
about fifty years ago these illicit bonds
in families of particles expressing forcefully
"You are a private investigator, a solitary
man not indebted to his employers.
I do not want my problems discussed with women"
and he was told to skip the wisecracks
searching for the material truth, hadrons
leptons & baryons, booze & cocaine
& about that time a private dick starts nosing in
so the Manhattan project goes ahead in the desert
cloud mushroom cloud nine cloud nix
it isn't the butler who does the murder
it's not that kind of story, it's dark & full of blood
to bring the war to a successful conclusion
in history they see Pluto's wartime significance
& privately decide to bomb military objectives
so intimately part of city life the big knockover
is lined up for homes turned to military use
with a licence for the gun to investigate
the dive singer blackmailed for the millions
by using the bomb the neutron projectiles
fused the lives of underworld characters
& many were saved while others were
just out on normal business in the street

Mendelevium 101

Everything is not made of parts. Desire has no end
except when you leave for work and think tomorrow
from seat to seat in one continuous element of list
all the beginnings in order to equate movements

the arms & head don't decide anything without.
Yet the molecular crystal idea holds free atoms
inside its polarised structure, until only one element
after another is defined as eternal angelology.

Satan knew all about deconstruction. Hell is
uniformity after the mental wars science
was captured by military appropriations and truth
shot and resurrected. Experiments could destroy

the elements. Fire wind earth & water were fictions.
After the death of love as god they were haunted
by the solidity of eternal matter from which there is
no vacation. Only artists painting one another for art.

An old photograph shows the first atom broken,
the solid world of god and state on solid elements
decaying at their push. And matter could be trashed,
the basis of the whole world could be disintegrated

no absolute, no permanence, no eternity, death
for all powers that stuck the world together death,
each atom, each godhead mortal in electrons
and a blizzard of charging bits. They named the element

and blew it up. Nothing lasts. Zero is best
for the scientific power to destroy ritual procedures.
What the corps de ballet of nuclear physics forgot
was the passing of time, the preserved production

had no audience, no love, no body.
The music changes. The dance changes. The body
grows and decays or becomes someone else or loves
and the materials of an idea are diverse as passim.

Fall Out Shelter

I think this poem will become more lifelike
from behind the fifties desk to desk linked
to Conelrad all America simulating the end.
Room intercom broadcasts the principal's
orders to the teacher's ear, holiday carpenters
have stripped away the scratched drawings
the wood shines again, varnish gives depth.
Carrying a tray of island foods to the shelter
of the desk, each rotary joint moves on separate
axes, for the time being are we going to keep
out of the radiation? Never remember this.
Read up on early pioneer days, see red
men in history, clear trees, distill the maple,
synthesise the suburb, the colour white house.
A jet defends us passing the sound barrier,
my smashed ear explodes into a co-ordinate
fear of axes, simulating rigid body parts
with my name preserved in the concrete
of a smooth sidewalk trusting the explanation
safely under a desk when the radio sirens
out into the free air, you hang a white sheet
flag in the window. Must we do the end now?
How to catch the bomb. You soften the glove
into a native paw, web the ball with a thunk
in your heart, a sting in the palm, survive
in the shelter, simulate the radio, live talk.
Run the sidewalk to a crossing monitor's yellow
yellow sash safety, teacher's voice is writing
and have almost arrived at school when the bell
goes and magnetic voices radio the new world.
It could never say you must change your life,
time to school, anticipate history, still and small.
No I cannot tell you how small history was then.

Up Above the Moral World

I don't want to imply that seeing Kennedy's
    gun carriage coffin roll by is a historical
    condition of ground control to president
Bush the moral category positioned within
    claims about the moral failure in working
    selves with oppositional defiance disorder.
I note the silent and evasive acoustic clues
    to different ways of men being unburstable
    once the naughty bits have been crimped.
Bush certainly leaves his mark on time,
    even the upholstery of Airforce One gives out
    rubber stud sweetness allied with massive slam.
I think, says Cheney, and the semantics flinch as
    the perfume of the finest American leathers
    brings weight and punch to low frequencies,
"the president said precisely what he wanted
    to say" by the sweaty press-up sense-making
    practice which belongs to another past.
Will he do whatever it takes, take whatever it
    invites him to pile on the power for high
    levels of the right thing to do?
Dumb beautiful ministers do we receive you
    with free sense as we breathe more
    CO_2 in payback time?

I tore up all my LBJ for the USA stickers
        too long ago to remember how it feels
        to see a bumper avatar or tears for the ABM
        treaty, but this is hardly the end of the questions.
However much I may have freely chosen my life
        if it turns out the whole history of company was managed
        by others (Bush the MBA) my life could not have had
        the meaning I found in it, so Robert Pippin tells us.
I don't think I understand the new theory of deep time
        yet (the idea that fossils are disconnected events
        of zero temporal extent scaled by millions of years
        between)
        not even whether this is the A, B or M series,
Although already I feel a stateless pang
        for the distance between one fossil time
        and another that I deeply mistrust, and the lemma
        that deep time scraps narrative fits this unease:
One hundred's eye and two fossils encompassed
        around seven hundred billion days of human
        consciousness and complex old reciprocity
        creates its own deep experiential spacetime.
From my own faith base in the rollback
        my bootsoles can't see if this is the right
        dirt nor if my face searching for expression
might do, or not do, from this ground.

High-Heel Boots
(i.m.David Monaghan)

You walked the streets a teacher whose ground plan coincides with
Poetic faculties of pre-shift light, and I became your faults:
Understanding, judgement and the myth we were now in transit
From transcendental employment. The salient hospital
A brewery, a copy of Phil Whalen in your velvet jacket,
Cannot find place to apply to appearances the coat of memory.

If it sought, your talk, no personal gain, it nevertheless enacted
    a poise only one can hold
While the troupe absent themselves from the audience's attention
Which I combine merely as I appear to myself, shorter
But longer in conversation, as now, carrying on its power of
    intuition,
Whilst across the city moorland looked down for knowledge
And the measure in turn was another decade back and that
    beyond more than the surrounding uplands.

I exist as more than my memory of you gone out over the land that
    city hardly knew
Fold inner objects. The special mode of expectation you talked into
    your aftermath
Exists as an intelligence which now looks back across the valley we
    have just crossed,
Dodging cars on the new junction, climbing the dirt track cut-off
Given by the understanding after some love and delay
Still less mere illusion, the lines you strode were hoicked out of
    you plywood partitions wise.

That this is how it must be, follows at an early stage of the
     argument,
But now must be shown and you search for the best cut
In for you lie entirely outside the carpeted rapport of
     confirmation,
Saying think as we reach the university, we come from the
     visible,
Spicer's not in the office he's somewhere out here on the street
     in beauty
A limited entitlement by which we are both determined by the
     you I cross the city with inductively.

Charles Olson

(after 'Second Release' in Unpolished Mirrors *by Allen Fisher)*

All the time he was telling stories
knowing himself measured
and not up to the task any more than a fisherman
his point that the knowing is not in the nets
the shoals the charts the market forces
the books on things unlike history, places
used the same recursive conceptual formulae
whatever the location the purpose anaclitic

kept getting figures, names
inevitable precision just a few guesses
at what had been happening

the heart back into the matter
otherwise abandoned as love might mutate
and the gene pool of methodology be drained
into the institutional record bank
which makes it even less needed for hands
to change money into a clasp on
whatever hungers that moment flower and refuse.

The only Gloucester left is around the cathedral tower
silhouettes in bright sky where gulls are nesting
built to celebrate one desire that tried to kill the rest,
and as for its people, some left for the new terra firma
that he would later try to show was a tributary of Oceanus
flood in lives from that collective storytelling
he told anecdotes as evidence for what else is there
for what else is there streamed over him
carrying universities, eternity, and primordial possessions
out into that epistemology of anamorphic replication
where only the working knowledge that knows desire
can find its heart's desire in heart's desire in clarity.

Intravention
for Peter Riley at 60

E. L. Doctorow explains in a 1977 essay, "False Documents," that "everyone in London who read *Crusoe* knew about Selkirk, there was intravention. a mixing-up of the historic and aesthetic, the real and the possibly real." It may be a misprint. Perhaps the novelist is mixing up the real and the possibly real when he replaces the expected intervention with his own intravention; or perhaps he has found one of those rare words, neither jargon nor slang, living enislanded far from the centres of the linguistic economy, that have not yet been discovered by the *OED* or *Merriam-Webster*, and it helped locate "the indwelling of the art in real life." He may even have thought he was inventing it, as did the psychologist J.Keith Murnighan who knew nothing of Doctorow, and needed an original word when he discovered ten years later that some organizational disputes are resolved by a third party, who is neither a mediator able only to advise the two parties in conflict, nor an arbitrator who will impose a result on them. This third party, like a poem intervening between reader and writer, may impose its own form on the conflict between them, or may help these disputants create their own resolution out of the materials of their difficult connection. The psychologists' history of the word as neologistic jargon in the journal of *Organizational Behavior and Human Decision Processes* (57, 387–410, 1994) is contradicted by a different history convened this May 2000 by an internet search in just 0.4 seconds, although still a long journey for the electrons indwelling in the system. It found, modestly admitting its uncertainty, "about 25." Some are certainly slippages of fingers on the real: A Rob Lacy told a Star-Telegram forum in Fort Worth, Texas on "Should there be a ban on human cloning?"–"Yes, I am TOTALLY AGAINST INTRUSIVE GOVERNMENT, but this is one that I place in the same catagory [sic] of Hitler's intention to Create a Super Race, which Does call for legislative intravention." Such unhappy inventions demand intravention—mixing-up the historic, the aesthetic and their letters. A few organizations are powerful enough to claim the word without hint of errancy. In the Canadian Broadcasting Act (1991), the Canadian government sets out the procedures if "the Corporation has contravened or failed to comply" with its own structures, like the poem which contravenes verbal associations or fails to comply with an initial metric, under the heading—"Report of alleged intravention or non-compliance by Corporation." The definition of poetry as intravention between writer and reader may not yet be a valid use of words, although even by this short passage intravention may have crossed the ocean threshold and become a full word. Let's hope so—poets live in hope of sighting such negations of singularity.

I Feel Your Pain

The houses were crumbling, it was Chechnya
without the war, ruin without the history, this long
alley of terraced houses with parts missing and raw
brick neatly stacked in zigzags. I kept walking.

Suddenly the lawns and finished houses of middle
class certainties opened on my destination, a Hegelian
who welcomed me by showing his neighbour's garden-
sized bed and the speculative proposition lying in it.

I don't consider this search for information over
yet, it is more a card catalogue to my reigning
preoccupations, a tree marking a tangled bank
of evolving life. There is only ever the story.

The victim of the Brighton bombing said she
could still walk in her dreams, she was never sitting
in a wheelchair, it was the Gulf without the desert
the peace without the mines. I kept wheeling.

Topologies

Portrait Of An Unknown Man

1

and he too was in arkady
where contiguous wars
plague slavery sexism
hemlocked minds
and the achievement of constant heteroglossia
dialectics and juries
are now dismembered parts
enabling parallels between otherwise thoughts
the structure does not possess a single straight line
of any length the deflection
creating an unusual dialogic
subtle convexity of columns
seen from either end
he was what i called a friend
anonymous and social as language
you're straight? never mind
it was contestable plato
said he was the morning
star now lights our evenings
there's a lot going down my friend
said he disappeared in the past i've also been
dismayed dead entombed graven latin
picture assuming
it's simply emotions i'm talking about
this is not an elegy
the boatman will always tell you when the last boat leaves
for your return journey

~

i'm in a beginning
workings black
blazer and coloured house tie
he didn't know me
and even on landing physical phenomena
not one but several islands
he bought three copies of zarathustra
for the binding shingle beach
noisy sheep cries bouzouki muzak
waves and pneumatic hammer
in as i write then
university travel work
displacement and see you
for a modern set-up of math
medecine art history drama and politics
he wrote me philosophy
was it orders from above
love or good social administration
he fringed this great civilization's
harmonies in gold
dopplering the glisten of trace wishes
where one construction is freely available
load bearing structures or frames
dominate
subtle variations make the city beautiful
women bare their breasts to the sea
while unaccustomed men occasionals listening
seem to be organising in front of you
it looks that way because it is that way
with all the complexities and mismatches
of mainstream epistemopoetics
its spring point is unknown

～

i want to facet
what he and he meant
by getting through the past
now i no longer see him
my friend jumped catching
the calculator as it dropped
toward the concrete 1980
long enough for the new conservative administration
to start rolling up socialism
barbarism was occasionally necessary to rejuvenate him
they thought discussion
indispensable preliminary to wise action
he believed in greek but spoke english
superabundance of intimate converse
driving out in his father's triumph
our self politics expected
enough to reverse the conditioned
dead childhood
in all existing state embitters
to walk and talk about books
on the hills above the town
of analogues and echoes
verbal traffic evolving
factored with fear
idea signs increased quantitatively
or trees or seas or rock
in the possibilities of thought
in or out of the deictic

~

beam me up plato
wrote a rough script to explain
a phase i went through of
getting everything down—
dreams history and sugar—
but now he works too hard to have dreams
he didn't always believe what he wrote
when i read the letter
what's so special inflated
his handsomeness about arcadia
he had theoreticals on goers and slags
on the women's sustaining he secretly needed
far had gaps
he bought a ford anglia to lie under
at weekends he called it athena
in fifteen years his letters became directions
acting up to interpretation
the fate of a star
emotional but not in person
understanding whose mass has
solar passages stepped ideas
masses was unclear
he wrote about his literature
abandoned friendships over differences
from mainland to mainland
that the intermediation lose enough
political transformation
during our lifetime in the form

~

2

sitting near the french windows
he went back to the exchange
of meanings sat down
and invented to numb out
humanist resistors
money before coffee
no one said anything about exchange
we played meanings
through slight shifts bubbling
the filter back in greece
the university began to move
her in with his contradictions
his flute girl could play
intimate associations
we breathed the piano near the window
stereo filled nights
with bach and the grateful dead
kept him always but
the new stereo philosophy
put firmly on the shelf at night
or creative works
equalled women for him
we sat in fawn deck chairs
all creative acts up a bit
yet suspended in conversation
greece in every act of interpretation
green and blue spines
spread ripples around the naval empire
of looking to the sea from athens
verbal response to high speed ideology
swamping the shore

～

he said each of us was responsible
for the entire goings on outdoors
as if isolated from the rest of the world
in his student life
delphi spread amphitheatricals
on the same basic then
you didn't hear the man near you breathing
if there wasn't a ceiling above
and a mattress on the floor
thoughtful silence
the science of lighting
up he committed his coffee
to the world of ideas
went to the delphic oracle
controlled by the known world
to affirm a future in his knowing self
he felt sustained by inexpensive leisure
reflection and stillness the sacred
valley telephone ringing
reminded us there was a connection
without the presence of men
a hand placed respectfully on the known
he said there was no delphi to be seen
not a conservatory only a room
abyss tripod clairvoyant
to fortify the improving graffito
evergreen yourself
to know pine
he hesitated then collapsed the chair
pythagoras liberated geometry
revealing skimpy substructures
that the real among the real among
the assigned departed starting forms
set different parts in resonance

~

discovered his ownership of voice
was mathematical harmony
inner power and present he said
she delivered his extravagance
but her theoretical prophecies
beyond intelligibility
had strained even his fortune
recording walkman he set
out for the east aggrandising
from the stripped pine top
he lifted a history
and the morality of the means
the philosopher discovered reasoning
systematically unreasonable
aphorisms on the long wave images
on tv he traced an underground idealism
back to fourth century athens and beyond
his shock was recorded
thousands of years away
over-determined energies mass
for many generations men have deemed
central deeming
as they moved newly worked observation
subservient to the organized
alleging fantasy toward
the end of my visit
our achievements dimmed to greek
extrapolations whose intangibility
opened the window to fundamental
serious warm june air from
sheffield steel works

~

there is total loss
of nerve and soul i sing
he called the nineteenth century
but knew better
euripides' fitted cave with word processor
aidos and theory it was hot outside
he said we must finish soon
fug lingered as he spoke
yearning initiates
she leaned in his
flute girl friend and went
modalities of touch and smell
argued the current girl
loved the busy festoon
kiss into this personal zone
green intimacy
left behind in the family's past
where there was plenty and imagine
a light and bodily green
cheerfully stripped pine doors
to enter the forbidden greek
empire of the sensorium
he said they got together about once a week
by professional conversions
abandoned kissing on the relationship
grain oil and designs for
a chain of love affairs
on the complex plane
had many persons involved persons
only two will mention me

≈

socrates asked again
what love is the desire for
his loons floated on
the oxfam mats and unswallowableness
impersonal penis
the intimate tongue forgotten
the exercise of dancing occasions
so equal a poise he wrote rare letters
with apologies at both ends
the lack this love displayed
what is it you mortals hope
to gain from one another
roach in the teacup
he said of his latest woman
if we know each of us
then the sex thing flies out the window
psyche's lure of longing
at last in mortal arms
passion gripped him
and he became his looks
for never can a fair
ruling be expected of a citizen
who lacks the apprehension of a father
understood at that time
in the imaginary and the proximal sense
he was surprised he got so much
out of the sanctuary
considering his leanings
performed regularly each year
eternity looking like art
toward anti-expressionism

∼

we were into the primitive
just out of university
the best amphitheatre in the machine world
built before ecology
the local god asklepios
scaring the sickness away
before the sixties
the new disease arose
equally divine and human
we visited the human bookshop
tourists briefly aware of a new reality
bump in answer to his query
said region where stars are formed
of supernova remnants
and other interesting exhibits
made me realise the harmony more
i hope he said the archaeological
gap position in nineteen seventy.

≈

3

i thought him secure
in his angry tie rods
inchoate feelings
of vastitude and new music
going out with her
he had written frequently from
where burning sappho loved and sung
from new york letters
i excerpt him a tenacity man
with girl friend along
he explained his centuries old grudge
long drawn out jaw firm obscurity
in terms of the worshipped glamour
of excess interplanetary transfer fantasies
poised between summation and forward programmes
in london he wrote about boundaries
of recognition maintenance
between designated familiarities
missed the new theatre and the return
to realism she was half america
survives copied down the ages
with a swift dexterity
different handwriting flares
left text in chaos

~

he wrote eternal summer gilds them yet
from the rhetorical cyclades
alexandria produced standard
hellish art movies
no spiritual compatibility
though nothing food
sex sleep alcohol can't cure
miasmas throttling across generations
he became a friend teaching children
young enough to be his own
childless he rolled
up his sleeve without
closely held friends
for all his close friends were lovers
to be heard in the perfect acoustic
of two
wanting to make himself sex
for absolution
very scary hims
shouting boisterously at
the ruins of a great entanglement
inhabited originality celtic
tribes funded london
commercial breaks
he bought this historic past
to flower paradise
tap spa

෴

he visited my desk and read my book spines
i found him change enhanced but wary
shook smokes out of a crush-proof pack
and offered impassive face
visible us
only want nature
like the broadest possible going
who playfully throws his colours
the gymnasium was empty
except for the two of us
he took exercise and wrestled me to
photogenic immobility
combined with the farmed nude male
military camps live
didn't know the secret then
to allow him so proud an exploit
the more open he
was the more secure
shaved off his sixties beard
several courses were set up as
an obvious choice for the beginner
imaging the unthought
between bashes
scan hence
more surface area to deflect
from his fashionable baggy cords
radio injections
without affection in the shoulders
without sexual expansion
in the stock market scene

≈

the mild era pretentiousness
developed to make him angry
to produce hallucinogenic technologies
like so many thirds
he stayed out of that century
disengaged all night
lived only in calendrical weeks
for style to follow the revolution
takes three generations
its primitivism he said
but it looks new born
i took him to the local pub
to distract him with you're
where you should be all the time
spreading ripples of verbal
male and female responses
to the constructors and resonances
of formalised masculinity
around each and every theory
that cultures british art
he was afraid of subjects
stretching from the waist not hips
all the way down neck loose
he drank the whole pint talking
then there was a silence
and i waited for more

≈

fortunately there are enough sexes
a seer was simply a person
with insight into the interpretation of signs
inity cannot question itself
the form of man as symbol
asking no questions drinking
earl gray later flavoured
with bergamot his girl friend
used in the bath
he said he was bored with
and left for the north
standing in my doorway
purely for familiarity's sake
the frontalis to
philosophical extensor longus
highly developed in man
fatherhood and chests
took exercise and unnestled me
attendant unchecked
gluteus and glistening rectus femoris
no longer matter they say
power equals beauty
he had done his part
despite staged binary desire
sex failed him
twenty-five years a man
with that code of women's bodies
meaning degrees of hope
from where what wherewithal?

~

he never cried
even when she left him suddenly
for men only dined together
with locked zygomatics in rigid countenances
malic moulds stamped out emotion
he confessed insistent desire
for women were lovely to him
and his incessantly stiff prick
he loved for its strong
self-assertive agon
from the upward age a man's duty
to increase the ordered understatement
when others bottle out
the direction from the east to the west
directly absorbing aesthetic rays
behind the past
friend you would think
glaring shines he closed
the window and turned back
the bed squeaked on his girl friend's side
and she had almost isolate hostile straits
in her whole length from his withholding
to clear from the beginning again
order he called for
who can feel a remark
in sensuous terms
brush its trousers against the kitchen table?
she had read his recorded history

≈

4

letters began to arrive in his absence
the view of social relations
shaped greek imaginative possibility
in the age of automotives
he was thirty going on four
his girl friend gave up on him
i learnt only incidentally
he fell into an emptiness of self
the difficulty lay in the achievement
of freedom from greek authority
art and epos
narcissistic disturbance
he underwent deeply felt mourning
for his hippy childhood
on the railway banks
and willow branch lines
still constituted a source and standard
of infinite attainment
but mourning restored vitality
endpoint depression
sitting on my stairs organising
the pages of his newest letter
he was able to say he was never
over several pages long
loved except for his attainments
in the childhood of society
evolved in the mail
didn't he enjoy the artless
translated ways of early evolution

~

his transit letters were enthusiastic
he might end one day
the courtship of narcissus
afraid of the intense psychotic
revival of every past epoch
as a child in the emotion
exerting eternal charm
from an age that will never
achieve lack demand
of his former fine child
the titanic on tv relay
in the pitch black respect
its stern broken tight
jeans and fairisle popover
reading him
tourismo against athens
when he went beyond freedom
from conflict as a boy it
concerned elm leaves grasshoppers
and mantis eggs hatching
nature in the classroom
he said he'd been an adult
since five
the spartan unwanted out to die
he'd been proper clever and clean anxious

~

he said he lived in constant fear
the ocean had withdrawn
revealing competition conspicuous
acclaim and wrecked forests of pine
disapproval ostracism
was a condition i couldn't imagine
he was out ten years
a huge sealed base
much more than in face to face friendship
so revealed replays
exporting surplus population
to the british and later american empires
he mentioned display charts
his first american teacher made in magic
he later learned was a marker
rejoined some severed nerves
while the walls we must have
of water to the sky watched the board
change states seeings
learned his fine marion richardson
italic script varying from black
cut to large strong slants
he could breathe underwater
wartime secrecy stops friendlies
he said i am feeling better
whether in the gymnasium
the pool or picture
most of the discharge
shook and shook
he laughed enough for two

～

he wrote in the comeback
reason is action
memory fathoming grace
saving weight i had deferred
responses out of idealism
and his self-timed exposure
then i told him the sea
was in place greece
warm and worn
with the founders and toys
from the new world he wrote
a letter full of placed errors
terrified like a calm sea leaching
constant smiles i recall now
as nerves and another golden age
metallically altering the command structure
before drowning at the feet of giants
the toxic sensors rend
through end his long disease
he wrote of the despair
raised by twenty four centuries done
since the end of pop assemblies
and rigid plastic fear of dying
despite the successful enlargement
of his back life
so angry with my decaffeinated research
he said every event became him
so cross-sectional of what went down
faulty layering
tidal wave loops in the fossil recording
heads set to metal

~

i stroked his face beside the mouth
at a distance
he spoke only of third parties
as childhood he'd given to neutral
objects and expressionist politics
i know that memory's the present's
lichenous amphitheatre
the old stone arcs managed impetuosity
built pasts changed these structures
wanting forever to be history
he conquered in only ten years
in and beyond the known
all that was left was to become a god
twenty-five centuries threatened with death
for impiety
he fled athens and seemed to drop
from the scene
was he still making records or
just scholastic cover versions?
he sent a photograph
which came out bent at the edge
casually dressed in macedonian cloth
i put on the larder door
a number one america he
knew the times for the words
thought fast about the world
he had no apologies to maintain
trouble was the stance held
by the break in thought
for holding his thought
he stopped hearing people think

∿

full of him are all the streets
full is sea and the continuum
lost to prose poetry and zeus
all denim blues in possibility
down through the water he went
layers and layers fresh and salt
until no form of thought inside
survived legend
as early men were
local clever persistently not gods
the element of beginning took him back
and the weather for that day dread
son of chronos
if we lie in a woman's arms
there is no safeguarding privacy on high
if one of the stars
of olympian athletics praised zeus
with convenient nakedness
that thou givest thyself to unto men
by instantaneous teleportation
and a trunkful of unworn blue levis
assuming the same taste for the next decade
faced with our mortality he wrote
immersion in the stream of relationship
lovers friends work politics art family
so deep death would be loosing
into the persistent element
remembered microcellulars
expansive subtle differentiated
and healthy racket he said
i edge along platitudes
and fall with startling oughts

∿

5

utopian vision on the road home
the problem is often called
otherworldly prime
squandering metal energy from lines
treated as objects and points to make
i found his letter on the hall floor
what is the bodily tolerance he asked
of high velocity doing duty
what is an orange for in england
his letter was written by computer
the future's universals half over
believing there's more there to be known
keep moving
another form of realism
don't believe the *guardian* he pleaded
with a new political tone based on
the plunged accelerator and quick
trips through the wing mirror ideology
that missed the mental adhesion
and sealed the universal up
he was living secretly in dalston
in position for the speaking subject he'd become
good prospects and particulars
he liked pubs and hated wine bars
agora discussion noise
barrier empire of reasoning
but the wine bar served good meals
and was still uncrowded at this late hour
in our friendship

~

cities of the system
barbaroi immigrants and slaves
share no common language
receive sign systems too weak to revolt with
the parthenon dominates space
where tropes arrive by boat
travel through ordinary space can proceed
at no rate more rapid than that of ordinary illumination
i wanted to know about his totaliser discourses
and he my position on struggle
asked me to leaflet the area
with general strike calls
on behalf of the miners
it wasn't avant-garde at all
it was as avant-garde as furniture
autonomy and internationalisation
located amongst the densely packed
barrel tables and chichi iron-work
populated with industrial advancement
he lectured on the ordinary
urban circuit internals
adjectival abstracts
glassed pine wealth's pluralism
and his demented analogue in the movies
in old business greys large and limp
supportive conditions for dissident groups
to sell carrier art

~

don't ask me what i mean
he would shout at the whole speaking people
it's all there on the mats of language
from slavery intellectuals are free
and slaves dead cheap
empirical silent ages of man
folded inward now lean
faced publication of the monument
the culture uttered between vast memories
meant years of travel between even the nearest
impossible travels except
through hyperspace unimaginable region
neither space nor time
one could travel the length of the universe
a traceable social factor
the city resurfaced in hyperspatial dimensions
until its radius was every street
the earth's unimaginable
devoted entirely to the galaxy over our heads
travel light he said
he became abstract
stabilised quanta of organisation
processed through our cellular culture
as we both ate cheese and onion crisps
the more the degree of human interchange
the more travel words do the more
the reach of thought
we had a row and he left

~

the ebbing tide of the empirical
family bank greece and dense ordinary matter
through the affective vacuum procedure
scientifically concealing the discovery moulds
as if the iron age meant iron
itself evolved swords and steel rollers
to make the bread white
for the planet where hurry and distraction
interfere with scholarly musings
and the cool production of progress
determine on the inside
the reforms of ephialtes
who gave athens the assembly
putting differences up for discovery
and emotional expression paid for
his reforms with his life
no substitute for co-extensive thinking
redistributed among the children the *ekklesia*
decided the rational everyone
was responsible and handled irrationalities
around the circle of discussants
start he'd said with sensible people
no pacifist dorks or junkie punks
leave round the clock activism
to trot cults
he now thought greek polity a failure
make sure you exist on earth
white society wants to belong to the question

≈

energistics he sneered
at my commitment to the new *isonomia*
middle class mutants
rich scum hands
poured out the last of the house red
this last time i saw him
both fists on the table
a blood-streak in his right eye
he said the new wave music destroyed early visions
and the looted tones dispersed
in widespread leisure damage
remember melanogenesis
even wearing a suit
mixed with all kinds of issue
trogging around london
working for the highly visible
inherent boys starved
eventual stone tiers composed
to steal by its very framing effect
turbined to challenge
engine discouragement
violently forth from purging anguish
british forth convergence tool
childhood elongated audition
expendable in organised fights
securing the sociables
soma man and slave
his new address card announced a child
he was teaching tough but good kids
and a year later he was a married
full time father worker campaigner
and out of some touch

∾

i know some thought these men a burden
feedback snarl pitched to distortion
impersonated affection gives
thinginess able uncanny patterns
sinuous intimacy and graceful limits
considered classicalness
left in an ancient world
floating all the way
while the spartan others had no art
but shields terrified men
pine has always been a favourite
with the help of stencilled patterns
gives the air a resiny smell
the elegance of our establishment
forms are a daily source of pleasure
fit you have to be fit
but he's been downed absented fighting
maybe this once friend's domestic confinement
the footing for liberation
as long as you live a common life
unsolved romantic

~

Sacred Object Purpose Unknown

As John the apostel hit sygh wyth syght
I syghe that cyty of gret renoun,
Jerusalem so new and ryally dyght
As hit was lyght fro the heuen adoun.
The borgh watz al of brende golde bryght
As glemande glas burnist broun,
Wyth gentyl gemmez an-vnder pyght
Wyth banteles twelue of riche tenoun;
Vch tabelment watz a serlypez ston;
As derely deuysez this ilk toun
In Apocalyppez the apostel John.

Pearl

'God sends a salvation city, the "City of God on pilgrimage through
this world" which does not exclude anyone . . . "a state of
unforgetting conviviality" . . . We should be renewing our thinking
on the invention and production of edifices, that is, cities,
apparently civilised within yet dominating without—not
sublimating those equivocations into holy cities.'

GILLIAN ROSE, The Broken Middle, Blackwell, 1992, pp.281–282 (citing MARK
C. TAYLOR, Erring, University of Chicago Press, 1984).

'As Schehezerade and Jesus both knew, storytelling can be a
powerful agent of personal transformation.'

JANET H. MURRAY, Hamlet on the Holodeck, The MIT Press, 1997, p.170.

1.

With blinding primary light back of you
go. Celestial identification is timeless,
a joy you must leave forever.
You eye the infinite ahead, sparks
curl in your visual field. They dart
and flash and die there. Who knows
what's beyond the beginning? Trainers
transport ready, complexes forming.
You cannot look back into the eye.

~

Leaving at the speed of light
an entire universe becomes you
backdraft angel, whose
line drawn hair waves goodbye
to the centre of the celestial past,
the usual end of story's welcome to endlessness,
and all the creator can do after creation's finished.
Narrative filaments hang from his mouth.
One city after another in the Empyrean's
gridlocked eternity, who else is enemy enough
to keep an absorptively moral plot on the up and up?

~

Have I been invented by the space
between the stars. Am I a decentred self
out in an induced trip's synaptic void,
a bargain Prometheus of pilgrim poetics?
The stars are recollective centuries apart.
No primary education kiss tag death
by stomach cancer's favorite teacher
Mrs Time cancels the cathexes.

~

The centre's rerun palace
made you earl for pages and dragons
in your millenial gold robes
and fourth century sunday best cope.
Favorites haunted the empire's eager funders
hollering futures, sill side of the exchange
overlooked by the pointilliste on high.
Semantic features ghost quoted investments.

~

Capital was tallness, goodness, looking
but not being self-conscious, strength
in prominences, a few isolated bright lines,
and its solar burden tied by atomic bonds
reaction shifting into sub torso carbon cycle rain.

∾

Infinite motes fall into this world
as monotheistic gene talk rises
for the duration of a cult trolley.

∾

In this container of all things transit
light is always the same light,
the past re-used to send new messages.
Keep the source behind you, aim
for the try out and hope raises
in person here is a fund manager
looking for start-ups with promise,
here is an academic and here is a child
each in designated building spaces.
Which do you really want to see first?
A little nervous, what will their faces show
if you examine them closely as they speak?

∾

Angels steam through the compartment
as it leaves the solar zone, falling back
from our utopian security
forces armed with kevlar insights,
once spray gunned over decades
to fade with rain and clean-up squads.
Slowly emerging from the system around
the central star, ranks of knowledge
lined up along its boulevards guarding
the emission of power and light,
a giant artist's wooden articulated figure
lurches out of the corona to hold you
back, to fold you back to plasma,
armed with reason, hold up the score,
and sing damn you, emote.

~

2.

In train are complex figures of
individual pre-history and pre-eminence,
travellers in cognitive ambience
to egalitarian seats in the flypast
from possible worlds
on the way to wake in places
too remote in time for you to ever see
or hear broadcast lyric grist.
Mental travellers hope
whose limits tend to infinity.

~

Commuters from all points of the future
and a costumed brain says where I come from
sex does not exist, this briefcase holds
my spare parts, memory deals,
zero seal loss.

~

Outside the window, hooped bodies wrench
mountain bikes across the pavement.
Look out, he's over on your right
running hard, he's going to, on these
unbalanced sidewalks, pay your stomach,
straighten up, graduate, and please
give generously to metaphysics.

~

Card of evening,
card of eye's lid
shading black light
to magenta, cyan, disguise,
neat slights, veering dread.

∼

History extends way ahead into the night.
Take that guy by the sabbatical window
He hails from far out on the spiral self.
Tribute ailments catalogue occupants
carrying duration, now what, what
would you do if pinking this figure?

∼

Anxieties hit at mathematically correct intervals.
Long term social change whiles away
the street, the catalogues, the empathy.
We are already different but economic inequality
travels too fast to compute. It is its own end.
The unconscious has many friends and expects
no one to mind unkempt hair, distributes
lucidity, remembers the oil and stripped hum
of dream people with the day on go.
Walks up and down the monad in magnetic shoes,
co-axial mind on other things, but tenants deny
he is a recluse, and outside, beautiful wasteland
drifts by clan transfer from winter to summer.

∼

There is too much noise from the engines,
cits reach for the earplugs on the long march
through a famous space with fictional looks.
Nova flotsam quoits trip you in the storm, salt sticks
to everything, passions drop to the floor
near a single rose delivered daily to an express
stranded in the west, ideal readers
half in love, half in a primitivist
seizure or pile-up of the continuum.

〜

I cannot represent any more of this civil life
on such a bumpy journey my dizziness overtakes me
with nausea and my stomach fakes orgasm repeatedly.
Cold long grass bent by a stream we hurtle past
the sky holding back infinity as only it knows how
and I feel I cannot bear to lose that grass.
Stand sway and shout to the car's absent passengers:
I am no ego you image of dead male after dead male,
I am no one night storm to prove you ungodlike at last
you shrill-toned smoke of terror's shoddy presence.

〜

Days between imperialism and natural history's
efforts to be colorful. Signs of morning buzzard over.
Cyclical time parasites dance in meiosis,
morning assets circle interest in the marsh
and need says something lost to clipping.

〜

3.

His education begins. He has read a book.
It was written by someone who was not him.
He hangs out of the institutional window gasping
cool air after marijuana has smoked out reason
tries to stop his penis from rolling into the hot air duct,
the back wall sees a nipple hide under the carpet,
his head shelve itself opposite the vessel
starting in the pelvic cavity, emerges at perineum
ascends brain to wind midline of the forehead,
while liver meridian curves to external genitalia
to pertaining organ the liver, an eye branches off,
and this body places itself at once in the several,
and like Orpheus lies on the celestial city map.

∾

Bussed to the outside world's
perceptual memorials of exemption,
fed from the reservoir of
electively what you do well
those apolitical pull-outs
as the years pass, don't you see,
days like problems detail
ethical ticketting, check,
slip, liaise, go on.

∾

The ratio of moving time
to industrial time
is sticky enough
for out of the body goings on,
like parliamentary consent,
or integration of the superego
several feet behind a laugh.

~

An experimental pattern that is cell automata
under the surface, morning sun hands answers
a few moments of selfhood, amid walkways
splitting into trip stains and rolling mercury.
The page smells of loan sweat and certainty,
monsters nanny us from their intestinal caves.
How often he reads for the incomprehensibility's
reassuring vesicles, roistering abstractions.

~

As he tightens his identity, the empathizer
looks in from Hollywood-on-the-muscle,
while his temporal gland sleeps fitfully,
nightmares of deracinated rhetoric
claw along his glottis, scraping mucus
off disconcerting English junked on guess.
He could be almost entirely other people.
A library is the biggest relationship of all
to those intelligences, sail hypotheses
clear the ground on a rising speculation
and caring palaeotype combs
representative unthought fixes
singing back new ideas from where
everything that ought has been said.

~

Writes each book at least twice,
once for the city and once the barbarian
horseback glamour, bright tents and each
evening the day rehearsed to the border
of the map, no unsung path, essence good
from the library window light travels on.
The world expands faster than history
and previously invisible stars wake you
at night, travellers talk openly
of the unknown, everyone is on something.
Romance of insight turns up the beauty.
What is the silence accumulating now?

~

Feels the ego carefully all over for damage.
Bits of consciousness rim the pacific, frayed
off his passing. Take the arteries
out of his heart, passion moves.
Therefore and thus counter bleeding
soluble colour in the field.
An art necessarily short
of eternity's drive shift.

~

Forensic gets a look at the statement
for personal threads not visible to the naked eye
of finite but large numbers of cells co-operating
to form persons for now, each dot of color
has its own space, look back in storm
and suddenly the lifejacket harness unhanks,
it was never used in poetry before
and tears free from the foresail,
sweeps the length of the safety line.

~

That was the classic novel on car radio-cassette.
Tyre shake eats the voice company
of men speaking endlessly mylar formalities.
He finally begins working with air,
that most plastic and necessary medium
of sealed site and halted erosion.

~

4.

I the traveller in these words testify
that this is a true record of what I saw.
I saw my great grandfather watermark the page
under carbon deposit letters from some
living there unconcerned he was trouble
polishing a sporting gun his factory made
idly along his trousered leg, his foot resting
on a piano stool while a woman played Schumann,
I said why to him, he was not really listening,
the sound of a voice in the garden,
he was my indifference to what happened
to his family when he died the father
of young children, I said something
I could not hear, this was only my art
you know, I could hear my own children
downstairs, why I said, this time
did you leave them all so bitter
and he showed me the gun which means
my friends would say the non-existent
conversation with him turns it all
round identities of the sudden.

～

The family works like a weapons battery,
the battlefront is deafening, sky tracers
join the lost minds, ravelling libido.
With an engine dummy.
Mother boiler's inside fire
without the addition of disfiguring pipes
or ducts are beautiful postmodern museum façade.

～

The right angle man's millenial sweep,
nail iron rusted, cross dressed, pardon high,
no thunder shaker, the maker disappoints
the children in his museum, unbenching
his millenial jaw in carved stone,
his dinosaur footprint cloud.

∿

Back this speech act over the event horizon
into the first minutes, a place on the line
out of the city to a nubbly bit of grass
in the everyday, a lord of light in presence,
and yet pass safely on to nominal predicate.

∿

5.

He begins life under a new name,
just him and the radio,
centuries of logic gone
in a few hours, people want,
it changes things, rusts solid planets,
people want to fly like griffons want
to be in this century, laughing off
surface in the smallest act of speaking
streaks of reflected solar magnitude.

~

Living in scribal muddle offers new temptations:
who swallows, who is one on whom nothing is lost,
who moves from one perception swiftly to the next,
who is too true to the moment, who unconceals,
who rises in his art, the art he creates will indeed exist.
he possesses his soul as the bull of the field
among the unnumbered stars without names
a recognised variant of the island of dancers.

~

But by now these easy chairs are sculptures,
non-existent, but posited as means to a proof,
and flashpoint wars lift on vertical jets
advances in recognition which span
the present with their outstretched hug.

~

Moral crises are run up quickly on the machine
and aren't always ablation products of much care.
They need all the returned's extraterrestrial
fractured spheres from deep ice cores
for ritual micrometeorites land wishes
like old cosmic dust on everyone's shoes and certainty.

∾

Reflective transportationn is a fiction
that lets the returned self grow smaller
piece by piece and stop, perfect, all scale
no size, relative to all things in this arrangement.

∾

And from rite to the everyday
he walks out alive leaving no logical
record behind, nothing the eternal city
can trace him with. Simply walks
out to the end of the words for eternity.
It's never this easy, but at least he is up on it.

∾

A Dialogue on Anachronism

This is no holy city we've ever seen.
We have left our old vehicle in a park
and ride determination well outside
the celestial city of ruched hills.
Portable screens collage angels
of data above the plaza, paper tigers
are so whitewashed they glare
in the enterprise zone neon.

Our hotel air-conditioning keeps out
these hot cries of post-equality.
We can see heritage side-streets
where dim bars add beauty moles
to the utopian razzle elswhere.
My partner intimates the future
will be no heavenly urbanisation
if she can help it, though she's willing

to converse with politic revision.
Suddenly the masters of theory glide
past our many stars on petalled floats,
looking like stuffed personifications
or imps of prosopopeia, their icons
show on the film as errors of surface.
I don't know about her, but I feel fake,
discomposed, unscholarly, punk.

Watching this gang show what's beneath
the waist of argument, I suddenly want
the towers wrenched from history now.
But she calms me interest free, saying,
these are goods, signifiers of manageable
change, admirable as self-governing
societies talking bear over the mobile
(though a pity about the retinal injustice),

and then horse carriages, motor cars,
helicopter gun ships, anti-gravity
fliers, and a couple of leopard skin
barbarians on foot, straggle past,
as my interpretations ebb to capital
and registered interests sense flat
path opportunities under the steel
arched trusses bracing mannerist limbs.

But then I suddenly lose it, shouting
I don't care about your spirit of die
for France, you essence of aid,
or you cater for differ ands from ins,
scraped skies are still political signs,
identity is more than this, and here
I stop, confused by the predictability
of these ejaculations, my undoing.

Club scruff cracks into my voice zone
as if it were already a ruin sublimated
by industrial pollution's masterly surplus.
Almost nothing of our love is now left
or so it feels, but I try one last gesture,
perhaps our basic humanity can be
irradiated to reach beyond its sell by
now the carnival's over and we can see

the sights: the old monoglot god's fortress,
the new museum of spirit, the market?
My thought and feeling fold neatly into
a guide book, but she who is after all
not my spirit, collects our floppy decades
of conversation and just walks away
across the shattered asphalt. Hey, I scream,
isn't that the man's Orphic role?

In desperation I film as mirrored tesserae
over her residual love, and the knowing
images modernise as she becomes a feminist,
I join the men's movement, she performs
her gender, I try to interface my quanta
with our cyborg selves only to short out
when she historicises, and then although
I cite a theorist or two, she sees through

what she calls my dead master strategy:
now only a third person (and in what
reference are all the third persons hiding,
they can't all be names on a memorial)
could possibly do what we don't know
and take all those pleasey words out
of polis the poem, and the hidden
hand of a joint narrative does take off.

What was that all about, she says
when our bipolar projection stops.
The trouble with poems is even
when you co-author the things
you're not sure what's been done.
Do we blame masters for soar
and crash, slip a word under
my wing and let semantics fly?

Without masters even democracies
of explanation can only trust
the other's hold on bits of new
fallen sky and soaring ground
can ever mean rights to love
such unfolding of exchange
to keep this ready to hand fakery
renewal enough to be and be.

I told you it should have been
in uniform style, I said, but she
laughed. It's just trying to confuse
us she replied, one moment out
to fuck your hole the next a passive,
or working so slowly around the vowel's
wet clitoris of sound, the rippling
consonantal shocks take you over.

We were very close there she said
there must be some more stuff
lying around, there's something
for everyone, from the new sent
to the old meta, serial topoi
and even the odd lick of flesh.
Bottom without bottom, drawdown
plash of bandwidth divers.

But the pastoral is on the gurney
she said, it votes with a credit card,
and philhellenistic aerosols
blotch its face, we've shocked it
many times but ventricular fibrillation
makes it harder and harder to find
any closed text left in this on-call
culture of carbon and debugging.

Isn't this poem way too strong
to sustain damage? Critical tailgaters
can be flipped off. He takes out
his mouth and holds it for everyone
to see: "forms, arias, puns, poetics,
copied at once by fashion chains,
they're what we have to resist."
The mouth drives off in a 4×4.

I am telling her to syncline
this fraud, keep the cosmological
under wraps, but I can almost
taste the millenia dropping away
Herodotus is on the local news
and his high ascension rating
furbelows the source. She says
I should realise the annihilate is left.

You can't dismiss the mock greek
stuff so quickly, she says, why only
go for the slammed auricular now?
Let's set up the frame of our house
not by simplifying simplifying
even if on-call society says the reverse.
A brick in her hand is a weight
of expectation, to build or break.

The problem as I see it now,
one says, is that the masters of
the verbals tried to make the city
of endings last into casting us.
And, she adds, we have to counter
story with story, the more fake
the better, there is so much past
to tree the flight of line art.

Afterword

The poems were written between about 1980 and 2002, their field of reference the political culture of the Thatcher and Major governments that abandoned all discourses of egalitarian social progress, and the manageralism of the Blair government which devalued art and idealism. Returned from Buffalo, now living in London, then Cambridge and Southampton. Times of high orthodoxy in literary and cultural theory, internally exiled modernisms, close communities of poetry magazines, presses, reading series. Beginning with a scientific poetics, writing through to a less system-conscious address. Poems are printed as they originally appeared with only minor alterations (with the exception of *Portrait of an Unknown Man* which appears in a different version to that published in *Temblor*, closer to its first composition), and I have not tried to mitigate angers or aspirations in the earlier work that now seem partially determined by their moment.

Started with belief in the possibility of a first poetics: otherwise untransmissible experience, and the analysis of knowledge's genes. Meanwhile the literary theory to which my colleagues daily renewed their pledges in the Eighties dismissed such beliefs as essentialism or idealism. Mathematics had seemed to proffer models of the world as symbolic pattern, barely capable of verbal rendition, and yet to that degree apparently embedded in the very phenomena they were trying to grasp because basic terms (point, set, number, greater, contained) had bits of the world sticking to them. A field of knowledge, physics, or mathematics, or sociology, could be then considered as an elaborate mechanism whose workings depend on the principles--axioms, key terms, central metaphors, dominant images, basic functions—which body forth an expression of the world. It seemed obvious that what needed investigation was the process of their choice, the efflorescence of such germinal concepts, and that poetry could do this, could take its restriction enzymes to work on such first principles.

Practice, however, lets in unwritten complexity in the divinatory elicitation of words jumbled in the day residues of consciousness, arguments appearing out of the archeology of semiosis, and voices calling from the vast blocky formulae in the massed anonymities of news texts, guide texts, memo texts, science texts, and classed texts. Unexpected thoughts and feelings litter the cities of the aftermath where narrative can be glimpsed in the radiation. This way, says the interpreter, is a route through the debris. Counter to the ubiquitous sciencing of the world, so much remains unexplained, unknown even in the immediate air and touch. Recombinant poetics is an organisation of unending social relations and not after all a specific form of discourse or knowledge.

The poems were written in conversation with the poetry of a few others who work in what Raymond Williams called "a zone of incomplete articulation". Some of this poetry has utopian aims, tries to achieve the reconfiguration of desire and its fufilments on which social transformation will depend, and is not simply an attempt to expose the shortcomings of the present, the failure of principles of equality or freedom. Such poetry does many of the things poetry has always done, it articulates the sacred, the passionate, and the otherwise inarticulable aspects of existence in the same room as materialist issues of knowledge, politics and textuality talk back. History opens the window.

England disappeared about sixty years ago although its requiem still draws crowds and sustains government ideology, and old ironies still persist as toxin decay products leaching into the linguistic ground. Assertion's story is told fitfully here and there in the new poetry, which tries to tell the scale of England's virtuality, its monochrome overlay images of empire, class placed people, and war damaged pyschic foundations. England may be the Lord Lucan of national identities, but it still has a lot to answer for, and many have been doing that and writing poetries which make its unknown a wider language than once seemed possible in the depleted political cultures of those years in the Eighties.

Notes

Divided By A Common Language

Lint, grey noise, and lecture asides from America in 1989.

Tell Me About It

Written between 1997 and 2001, first published by Barque. The poems consider the many selves which move through us daily. Newspapers, television news, cinematic drama, novels, poems, recorded music, and other enlistments of our cognition and feeling, work to coerce identification and consent with their presented characters and images, and sometimes demand emulation or deference. This could be considered to be a poetic critique of the theory of ideology as interpellation.

Paternalisms

Written in the early Nineties. Sections also appeared under the title *Is There A Male Language*, an allusion to Deborah Cameron's critique of poststructuralist theories that the phallus is the fundamental signifier, making entrance into language possible.

Portrait Of An Unknown Man

Written in 1985, a photo-fit autobiography made from anecdote and memory of various men and women, insinuated with gender theory, and infused with first attempts to decode passages of childhood and seeming exile in Washington D.C. when my father worked for NSA, the decoders of the communications of otherness, in the late fifties and again in the mid-sixties. A collected biography of those who came of age around 1970 and again at the end of socialism in the eighties, and their laconic intellectual abstraction. Marx said Greece represented the childhood of civilisation, and the poem treats Greece as a scene of individual childhood whose adulthood is our futures, political, emotional, intellectual and hallucinatory. The poem as a whole was an attempt to show how difficult it had become to think of oneself as having an articulable history and locate "what he and he [I and I] meant."

Sacred Object Purpose Unknown

Life as a journey—this is one of the main examples of a fundamental existential metaphor used by the linguist George Lakoff. Life as a pilgrimage to the Eternal City is a central Christian allegory and hence one of the underlying metaphors for our understanding of time. The poem traces a return journey from Heaven/Dioce/Olympus and their various Saturnine Father gods and astronomical glories, to the mundane. Journey's narrative time is imagined as temporally heterogenous, a non-place when people from many times and places are somehow able to meet and mingle in the cosmological unconscious.

Printed in the United States
1420900002B/174

9 781876 857639